E-COMMERCE WITHOUT TEARS

E-COMMERCE WITHOUT TEARS

PUTTING THE E INTO REAL BUSINESS

Naomi Langford-Wood

& Brian Salter

An imprint of Pearson Education

London · New York · Toronto · Sydney · Tokyo · Singapore · Madrid · Mexico City · Munich · Paris

PEARSON EDUCATION LIMITED

Head Office:
Edinburgh Gate
Harlow CM20 2JE
Tel: +44 (0)1279 623623
Fax: +44 (0)1279 431059

London Office:
128 Long Acre
London WC2E 9AN
Tel: +44 (0)20 7447 2000
Fax: +44 (0)20 7240 5771

First published in Great Britain in 2001

ISBN 0-130-89732-9

British Library Cataloguing-in-Publication Data
A catalogue record for this book is available from the British Library.

10 9 8 7 6 5 4 3 2 1

Typeset by Mathematical Composition Setters Ltd, Salisbury, Wiltshire.
Printed and bound by Biddles of Guildford and King's Lynn.

The publishers' policy is to use paper manufactured from sustainable forests.

CONTENTS

INTRODUCTION

They say that e-commerce is like teenage sex. You wonder what it's going to be like. You wonder if it will hurt. You wonder when it will happen. You wonder how long it will last. You wonder if the earth will move. Will it put you off for life?

You wonder if others will laugh at you. You wonder if you'll be able to tell your friends. You wonder how long you'll be playing around in the dark. You wonder if you'll be able to fulfil your partner's expectations. Your parents worry what it will do to you.

But it's going to happen anyway – so why not just enjoy it?

Let's take a look at what that really means. In society and business there are basically two types of people. We all know them:

- those who manage what they don't understand
- those who understand what they don't manage.

What we're looking at in this book are the new business processes enabled by Internet technologies. In those processes, and the ultra competitive global market we're in, we'll find that there is plenty that needs managing – and equally, plenty that needs to be understood. After all, a mere four years ago e-commerce was thought of as the brave new world. It was spoken of in almost hushed tones. Now it is the norm.

Very few people realised, and even fewer predicted, that e-commerce would be part of normal business. Not many people stuck their heads above the parapet or pronounced it from the rooftops. Not many people even tried to help their companies to get ahead of the game by developing an Internet-based commerce strategy. No one, after all, would have thanked them for getting it wrong, and it's a brave soul indeed who sticks his neck out only to get his head chopped off by those who have 20/20 hindsight.

And yet change is normal. In fact change is the status quo.

When people say that they want to maintain the status quo they usually mean that they want to keep the familiar around them. What they really mean is that they don't want to change, that they are scared of change or worried that they won't be able to cope with the new things that change brings.

But change – and even chaos – are absolutely normal states. The world is made up of states of apparently static periods that are broken by states of chaos. In fact there is no static period at all. Being static is an illusion that lulls us into a false sense of security and into inactivity.

The jerky transition created by the Internet, as it sweeps relentlessly through industry and the world, is like sailing in very choppy and discomfiting water. Experienced pilots cannot be found. There are no precedents.

People who have the knowledge are in very short supply. People who have the vision often don't have the business experience or connections to make a business model entirely credible or viable. The eddies and flows that the Internet produces have far-reaching effects. The scouring out of the traditional bastions of business and processes is taking place day by day, hour by hour – and reinventing the way that life and work is undertaken.

The relationships are all changing too. Some will go topsy-turvy and the norm will sometimes even become the opposite of what it was.

This is all extremely unsettling and, potentially, very dangerous indeed.

Forward planning is absolutely crucial if a business is to survive and serve its customers in the future. It is crucial if the business is to have customers at all – let alone make a profit.

For the Internet changes everything. The Internet changes the way we work, and it changes the relationships we have with customers, suppliers and partners, communications – everything.

In this book we look at what e-commerce really is. We'll cut the hype, disperse the fear, and, through examples and case studies, try to show how we can survive and grow whilst taking advantage of this amazing facility – as well as understand what we will surely have to manage, and manage what we have to understand.

PART 1

HOW WE GOT TO WHERE WE ARE

1

IN THE BEGINNING...

E-commerce would be nothing without the Internet. No, that's not quite correct. There is EDI (electronic data interface, otherwise known as electronic distribution of information) and various other peer-to-peer networks that have allowed e-commerce in a limited capacity to operate for some years now. But the coming of the Internet effectively brought e-commerce to the masses. In May 1998 *Computer Weekly* wrote:

> The typical customer has a clear image of e-commerce; that is shopping on the Web. It encompasses both business to consumer and business to business transactions. The logic of e-commerce is inescapable. It provides a world wide presence with low shop front costs. It reaches affluent potential purchasers. It is a sexy option for investors and it can give customers unparalleled convenience.

Only a few years later that definition appears simplistic, to say the least, because e-commerce has moved on a great deal in a very short space of time. And in the process it has transformed traditional business models to such a degree that a time-traveller from only 20 years ago might well feel totally out of their depth at the scope, speed and ubiquity of the new trading environment.

E-commerce is a way of doing business using the Web as a trading medium. But that definition barely scratches the surface. In real and economic terms, what does it mean?

Simply that e-commerce in particular, and the Internet in general, rely on the concept of networks. Without the values of a network they would be worthless. And that is why having to rely on proprietary EDI networks with their huge expense and limited reach meant this was purely a game for the big boys.

If one looks back in time to Ancient Greece and the Roman Empire we can see that part of their success lay in the communications networks they set up. Whether a runner brought the news of battle from Marathon, or a horseman travelled to Rome with the latest news of Boadicea's unruly citizens, it was the network of runners and horsemen that allowed central government of whatever type to make decisions and to import the wealth of their empires into the very heart of their societies.

It was also the setting up of the logistics that followed in the wake of the fighters looting, raping and pillaging that created an infrastructure to ensure that food and other supplies reached the armies, the injured were dealt with, and trading was established within, from and to the conquered areas.

A few hundred years later Queen Isabella of Spain sat in her palace and directed operations over on the other side of the world in South America, where her armies went in search of gold and other precious commodities. Isabella never left Europe, but because of her network of messengers, and the infrastructure set up by her invading armies, she was able to get a very clear picture of how her 'business' of government was coping and its bottom line. The ships might have taken an age to carry her messages to and fro, but she certainly knew a thing or two about managing remotely.

The coming of the railways in the nineteenth century brought a major leap forward in the networking of communities. The easier physical movement of goods and people – and the electronic telegraph – made a huge impact on the way society operated. With the railways came the concept of universal time for the masses, since until that point it didn't really matter if clocks in, say, Bristol or Penzance were set differently from those in London or Norwich. But if timetables were to mean anything at all, and with telegraphic communications allowing virtually instant communication, standard time became common wherever a new railway line or telegraph was set up.

In Surrey there is a well-known garden centre called Waterers situated in Windlesham on what is now the A30 near the town of Bagshot. Back in the 1840s it was in the middle of nowhere and was known as being a quality purveyor of American shrubs (rhododendrons in modern parlance). Who, apart from the locals and those on the coaching routes, had heard of Bagshot in those days, let alone knew where it was?

But then in 1857 the railways came to Bagshot and Waterers grabbed the new opportunity with both hands. Now it was able to deliver American shrubs to a very much wider clientele than it had been able to previously. And not only was the delivery area extended considerably, but the shrubs arrived faster – and therefore were fresher and less prone to damage by the time they arrived at their destinations.

Within 12 months Waterers had increased its turnover by 400 per cent simply by taking advantage of the new network created by the coming of the railways.

Fig. 1.1 Nearly 150 years on Waterers is taking advantage of another new network

With hindsight it is easy to see what it had done; yet at the time it took a completely new mindset to work out the business processes that could take advantage of a new situation and make the company more profitable. Think of the logistics involved and the redesign of their whole supply chain simply from the coming of the railway line through Bagshot. Also, plants do not grow from cuttings overnight, so they had to step up the production three years in advance of the first steam train pulling into Bagshot Halt. What a leap of faith and vision!

The railways gave Waterers a fillip and moved it up a gear. The benefits of speed could not be overstated. The existence of a new network became crucial to its business success.

Forty years on, the telephone made its debut. There is the oft quoted story of Thomas Edison going to give a demonstration of this new-fangled machine to the Mayor of New York. (The story may be apocryphal, but never mind.) You can picture the scene. In one room sat Edison hunched over his apparatus talking into a mouthpiece and, some way down the corridor, sat the mayor bemusedly listening to an ear piece from which he could hear the inventor's words.

After the demonstration Edison is said to have walked back into the mayor's office and proudly proclaimed, 'Mr Mayor. Just think of it. In a few years time using this apparatus, you will be able to speak to people over 50 miles away!' The mayor sat and pondered this information for a while. 'But I don't *know* anyone 50 miles away,' came his considered reply.

So Mr Mayor obviously missed the point. But it was not a point that was missed by many others. Today life seems inconceivable without the use of the telephone – we all take it totally for granted.

Those of us somewhat longer in the tooth can clearly remember that it wasn't many years ago that we had to ask the operator to dial us a number in a different town; and it wasn't until the 1980s that international direct dialling really came into its own. Nowadays with mobile telephones even being used in the school playground, it will not be long before almost everyone on the planet will be 'networked up' to one another.

So why are going on at great length about these different networks? Well, it was Robert Metcalf, the founder of the Ethernet company,

3Com, who one day made a casual observation that has been reworked into what is now known as Metcalf's Law:

> A network increases in value exponentially with the addition of each new user.

Or to put it another way:

$$(\text{network value}) = k^*(\text{number of users})^2$$

In other words, if I have a network with only one computer on it, then when I add one more user the number of users doubles, but its worth has quadrupled.

When Edison showed off his two-person phone network to the mayor, a casual observer might have been forgiven for thinking 'So what?' But with today's international phone network, not even the most cynical would deny its usefulness. The phone achieved critical mass a century ago; now, with the coming of the Internet, e-commerce can be said to have achieved its critical mass – its value is unquestionable.

So the coming of the Internet was critical to e-commerce achieving critical mass. But when do *you* think most people (in the UK, at any rate) first experienced e-commerce?

Surprisingly (for some) the answer is way back in the mists of time – well, in 1984 anyway. In those heady days in the reign of Margaret Thatcher some financial institutions got together to establish a Link machine network to allow people to withdraw money from their accounts without having to queue up to see a cashier. The cash machine – or 'hole in the wall' – was born. The banks quickly followed with their own ATMs (automated teller machines), and within only three years 'holes' were to be seen in every high street.

Only three years? It seemed amazingly fast at the time; rarely had a network established itself so quickly. But as we'll see very shortly, we hadn't seen anything up till then. The arrival of the Internet was different. It was like a dog ...

2

USHERING IN NEW BUSINESS PROCESSES

The Internet is different from the other revolutions that have shaped and reshaped life and business. The Internet is interactive. The speed of take-up across the demographic divides was not predicted.

They say that the Internet is like a dog. One normal business year is equivalent to seven Internet years. The take-up is that fast and eclipses everything that has gone before.

Tried and tested processes, business models and traditions have been swept aside. In the traditional business model, the biggest budget spend was on:

1. people
2. transport
3. IT.

However, with the advent of the dot coms it changed to:

1. people
2. marketing
3. marketing
4. marketing
5. IT
6. finally, poor old transport.

Because of the new ways for companies to get to market and people to reach the products and services, marketing was needed to raise the awareness of not just what was on offer, but how to access it as well.

The marketing budget of many Internet-related businesses has been higher than most traditional businesses would have ever thought reasonable. Now many of the original dot coms have overspent on the marketing and the traditional business model cognoscenti are reviewing the dot-com model so that the dot coms are expected to make a profit too.

Eventually, using the Internet within and without a business will become the norm and the size of the various budgets will adjust accordingly.

If we think through the process of ordering, some potential 'one-touch' processes can be seen clearly. When receiving a customer's order by telephone, fax or on paper there are always time-consuming and input-heavy systems to be gone through.

Within many computer systems – both from the big mainframe days and then within mini-computers before the PC became the norm – there were processes that fed through from order entry to sales: invoicing, sales and nominal ledgers, picking lists, dispatch and, on the other side, reorder of component parts and stock control; and they all required a variety of levels of input.

Now, however, it is possible for a customer order to come through on-line and for all of the processes to be automated. So, in effect, the customer is doing all the administration – well, once the system is in place.

This brings us to the knotty problem of speed. If someone can order on-line today, then it is quite likely that they will want to receive the goods tomorrow – or even tonight. 'Despatch within 28 days' is simply no longer good enough. Ease of ordering creates a customer expectation of ease of delivery. This has been a real problem for companies who have sorted out an easy ordering system only to fall into the trap of not being able to fulfil the order – and the customer's expectations.

Offices are becoming more virtual everyday. For instance, for some time now surveyors within local councils have often worked from home, only logging on to access their up-to-date diary of appointments. Many people do not have a desk or space in an office allocated especially for them anymore. 'Hot-desking' is the norm. Mindsets change all the time in order to accommodate this sort of change. After all, with a laptop or with just an identifying log-on, your computer desktop can be at your fingertips anywhere within the confines of a building, extranet or intranet – which also means that you don't have to get used to new surroundings or different machinery and software whilst being on the move.

Mindset changes are usually the more difficult to master because we all get used to particular ways of working and where our bits and pieces are. Time, therefore, has to be allowed for people to grasp ideas and adjust their mindsets to accommodate the changes that arise daily.

The high street banks have tried very hard to make customers do their work for them. In fact it seems that they have led a revolution in anti-service. It began with automation when, instead of keeping all the ledgers in the branch, the transactions were prepared and sent off to a computer centre. This automated much of what the banks did, and in the process did away with local cheque clearing and other time-consuming but time-critical processes.

The banks' customers found that automation had its drawbacks because, whereas they had been able to go into their bank branch and be shown their actual ledger sheet and statement on demand, the involvement of the computer centre added another process. This delayed the transactions, and statements had to be sent out from a remote site by post – customers had to wait for three days to receive their statements.

Customers can now phone their bank, get through a call centre (if they remember the various codes and security checks) or find out their balance on-line. Or they can print out a statement in the branch when swiping a smart card. On-line banking from a PC or through a TV set now puts customers in charge of their own banking – whilst the bank charges for things you do and forget to do! So the model is not really customer-focused yet.

What do customers want, after all? Do they want to be bank managers or do they want an advisory or personal service? When looking at new business processes it is essential to see it all from the customers' side – otherwise you could end up with some beautifully automated business with no customers.

Within the realms of Internet-enabled businesses many of the early starters got it wrong. They paid the price for being first, but then this often happens to pioneers. Someone has to take the first step on the revolutionary path ...

3

WHAT IS E-COMMERCE?

Let's cut the hype and define e-commerce as it really is – warts and all.

E-COMMERCE IS SIMPLY THE AUTOMATION OF PROCESS AND COMMUNICATIONS, LATTERLY USING INTERNET TECHNOLOGIES.

That's all!

So, in theory, if you can identify the processes that take place within your business you could automate many of them and make them faster and cheaper. You could perhaps even do away with some that are traditional but not necessary.

> **Essential-e** 'Any company that does not see this technology as important as breathing could be on its last breath' (Jack Welch, CEO, GE).

4

SWOT!

A SWOT analysis is the first, and meaty, step toward the achievement of a viable business – beyond that of having 'the idea'. Just because a business is Internet-enabled doesn't mean that it shouldn't have a business model that cuts the mustard.

It is quite amazing what a properly conducted SWOT analysis can reveal – both in upsides and downsides. And it often surprises people how useful a SWOT analysis can be, in that it forces people to consider what they might well have overlooked in the rush to get their 'baby' emblazoned on to the doors of every London cab.

Firstly, let's look at what a SWOT is and then what the objectives are for doing it at all. Most people who have started a business know well that their backers will invariably ask them for a run-down of its strengths and weaknesses, opportunities and threats. (They may not call them that, but that's what a SWOT analysis is by any name.)

You don't just do a SWOT analysis when you are starting up a business; it should be part of the on-going forward planning of any company.

There are basically two ways to approach a SWOT – one by committee around a big table and one where each member of the team (both internal and external) answers the questions individually before coming together to brainstorm it through in a strategy and planning meeting. (We always find that a couple of bottles of Chardonnay and some Pringles invariably jolly the brain cells along to impressive and useful results.)

If you are intending to Internet-enable an existing business, then it helps to look at that in isolation first – to ensure that you see the business clearly and don't confuse an element that is essential for e-commerce but not needed at all within the terrestrial one. After that, looking at the e-commerce and Internet side will identify the pluses and minuses within this area very clearly indeed. A look at the individuals you have identified to be working with you is also essential – just as the company has strengths, weaknesses, opportunities and threats, so too do the individuals.

The first thing to do is to look at the functions that have to be fulfilled in the business and then ask how you are going to fulfil them. It is most important at this stage not to kid yourself that you can and should be able to do everything. There are too many role misfits where directors of small companies are almost into self-flagellation – assuming that they should be able to do everything rather than sticking to what they do best and letting others with different areas of expertise cover the work in those areas without any feeling of guilt.

Using the following series of questions is a good way to prepare everyone to start thinking towards your common goals. (You can download a copy of this SWOT questionnaire from **www.e-biz-pro.org.**) Once each team member has individually completed it you should hold a strategy planning meeting with them.

Strengths

- What does the business do very well?
- In which fields is it an acknowledged leader?
- What are the business's greatest assets?
- What is its USP (unique selling point)?
- What was the business's greatest competitive success last year?
- Is the business well placed with new offerings with which to keep the competitive initiative?
- Will, or does, the business have strength in an Internet presence?

Weaknesses

- In what areas is the business weak or deficient?
- What are the business's greatest liabilities?
- What were the business's greatest failures last year?

- What was the most important competitive loss last year?
- How badly placed is the business to respond to competitor initiatives?
- Do you have the human resources and infrastructure to cope with the world of e-commerce?

Opportunities
- Where do you think the business's main opportunities lie in the next year?
- Does the business have any significant unexploited physical, financial or intangible assets?
- Does the Internet offer the business an opportunity to save costs?
- Does the Internet offer the business an opportunity to provide better customer focus?
- Does the Internet offer the business an opportunity to be more efficient?
- Does the Internet offer the opportunity to reach new markets?

Threats
- Is the business significantly short of human skills or capabilities?
- Does the business operate in markets where it has an inferior or uncompetitive position?
- What new competitors have entered the market or become significant over the past year?
- What probable or possible changes in client organisations, markets or industries could constitute a threat to the business?
- Are any of the business's markets reaching the size where they will attract the attention of new powerful competitors?
- Do you see any other significant threats to your organisation's business?
- Does the Internet offer others an opportunity to poach your customers?
- Does the Internet offer others an opportunity to gain industrial information on your business?
- Does the Internet offer others an opportunity to make your business uncompetitive?

Being honest about these difficult questions at this time will save heartache later when your Internet presence has built a momentum all of its own. Don't forget that when you look at the skills that you and your team have it is important to see each others' strengths and weaknesses in a true light. Identifying these now will enable you to see strengths and weaknesses that are inherent in all teams and then enable you to build on that knowledge.

Having a weakness is not an offence; it is something about which Wol (or Owl) of *Winnie the Pooh* fame would have had the opportunity to say, 'No blame should be attached to him.' By looking objectively at everyone's strengths and weaknesses, a stronger team can be built.

Meredith Belbin's analysis of team roles can help considerably here, identifying the different individual traits, strengths and weaknesses. There are companies who are licensed to run Belbin tests through computer analysis, so enabling people to see what they are and are not good at. This analysis also shows combined strengths and weaknesses of the group the likelihood of success or failure of the team.

An example of how the use of the Belbin test persuaded some business people not to go into business together occurred when a trio of business folk got together to explore the possibilities of forming a dot com venture. They decided, having spent several mornings over several weeks, that they were getting nowhere fast in their deliberations. As a last ditch effort to try to put a finger on the reasons why, one of the trio suggested running themselves through Belbin. This showed that two of the three were identified as what are known as 'resource investigators' and the third was a so-called 'co-ordinator'. The three people had the technical and Internet expertise, but there was no one in the team who was a natural 'completer finisher'. The likelihood of success for this trio was not high unless augmented by other people who were naturally inclined to fulfil other functions (and on top of that there was one too many 'resource investigators').

This does not mean that they could not have set up a successful dot com business, but it would not have been as successful as one that had a complementary set of skills within the team. You can always do work for which you are not ideally suited, but isn't it better to do the things you are best at and find others who can do the things that they are best at too?

Once you've SWOTted away you'll be able to avoid some of the costly mistakes that have been made by the front-runners on the Internet-enabled route to success.

PART 2

GETTING TO GRIPS WITH TRANSITION

5

SWISHING THE BUSINESS MODELS

To see any of the lessons learned during the current short and bubbly transitional stage from 'traditional' business towards Internet-integrated business we must first issue a truly global warning to business people everywhere; global, because – in theory – the Internet makes every business accessible from anywhere else on the planet and it also opens up a global marketplace for every business.

Conversely, the Internet also opens up global threats to every business that may think it is safely ensconced in its own home town and won't even see the predator coming. It is like an out-of-country predator that can snaffle customers from under the businesses' very noses.

Because of this, business planning needs to be brainstormed out of 'wild-thought' territory and then be brought down to earth and planned into reality. Quite a lot of business models have been devised (according to tenets), but because the Internet is different, they were wrong in themselves. History identifies successful and failed businesses as well as the basic networks that create the infrastructure needed for them to survive, trade and grow.

How many times have you heard those prophetic words 'think global, act local' repeated by management and e-commerce gurus ad nauseam? But the concept must be grasped if a company is to reduce the risk of failure – whether bolting on an e-commerce aspect to its business or launching a totally Internet-based entity.

Let's take a look at the reasons for this global warning in a marketplace where anyone can trade from a garage in Penge, a bedroom in Otley or a home office in 'downtown cityscape Islington' with equal aplomb (or lack of it).

Who'd have thought it? We even came across a dot com company that set up shop in the Wharfedale Valley and promptly sent out a press release identifying West Yorkshire's new Silicon Valley!

Looking at a map of the world there is no reason why you can't sell directly into New Zealand or even Japan. Well, in theory there isn't, but in practice things are a bit different. Customers may well be found for your goods and services, but good communications also need to be built from nothing, whilst infrastructure, support and customer relations need to be available.

Getting your goods from A to B could be too costly and could prove to be a backbreaker when it comes to profitability. Time-zone coverage could mean that you have to staff-up for longer shifts; and in even more basic terms, the reliance on some of the technological equipment that underpins the Internet – telephones, televisions and computers – is not accessible in large parts of the world. There is an unequal distribution of the nodes for access to the Internet that makes some apparently plum target markets full of the type of customers you're chasing just unviable – the term 'global' is simply not applicable.

Foundations Internet node distribution in June 2000:

Some five million nodes globally, of which 3.4 million were in North America, one million in Western Europe, 200,000 in Australia, 150,000 in Asia, 46,000 in Eastern Europe, 27,100 in Africa, 16,000 in Central and Southern America, and 13,800 across the Middle East.

Demographics and population clusters (together with language and cultural differences) also need careful consideration before you can

Fig. 5.1 Terra ISP is likely to boost Spanish language usage on the Net

expect to take on the world. At the moment all things Internet are dominated by the English-speaking world and its cultures. However, don't forget that China is up and coming as an international trading nation, albeit that it is held back by having only four Internet nodes (at the time of writing) and a complicated language (at least as far as the rest of the world is concerned!). Spain also has a growing presence in Internet matters since Terra became the biggest Internet service provider (ISP) by merger in the spring of 2000.

The power and balance of the use of languages on the Internet will change. This will drive the need for automatic translation engines that will ensure the ability for all to communicate with one another. These issues apart, there are knottier problems when you intend to trade in different countries, which are the result of jurisdiction and custom.

For instance, Lands' End, the clothing merchants, was forced to withdraw a guarantee (which was valid in other places where they had an established mail-order business) when they started selling on-line into Germany because it was contrary to German consumer law.

Fig. 5.2 Lands' End had to think global and act local

Local issues therefore need to be understood and addressed for all the territories in which you intend to trade even if this means administrative complications and adjustments to satisfy local needs around the world.

Think global but act local is the key to success – a concept that is simple when still thinking in the theoretical plains but more difficult to grasp at the practical level. For example, in a national advertising campaign it is simply not sufficient to expect local take-up in someone else's local-focus game.

This is one of the new ways in which businesses need to be planned – which skews the tried and tested business models that the financiers and entrepreneurs have long held dear. The key is to be a good ordinary business that harnesses Internet technologies in order to give it extraordinary advantage. Exploiting the Internet is essential in making your business more efficient and to really look after your customers, as well as deliver better products faster and in better condition.

After all, the dot-com bubble bears similarities to the housing market boom of the late 1980s that led to negative equity situations in personal lending and expectations. The over-hyped and misunderstood Internet-enabled equivalent is bubbling along in a similar fashion, showing violent share valuation changes and current share prices well below that of their offer prices at initial public offering (IPO).

> **New model, old statistics** Half of all new businesses fail within their first four years and the death rate for dot coms ought to be even higher. Clickmango.com was notching up sales of just £2000 a week – 'corner-shop stuff' as the *Guardian* (August 2000) described it.

And, as with houses, some are good and some are bad; some are in good areas and some not so good. The only way to sort them out is either by having the expertise with assumptions based on a good business model, or else because the technology is so cutting-edge that you have the expertise and the vision to ensure that the business model stacks up in all other areas.

So, the best way for most of us is to look at our existing (or hoped-for) business and see how we can best exploit the technologies to give us that cutting edge and market advantage that others will not have been brave enough to take – or knowledgeable enough to envision and grasp.

The net effect of e-commerce has yet to be seen. If a process can be automated using Internet technologies then costs can be saved and prices reduced. This, however, gives a short-term advantage. Many will follow the example set, for instance, by Egg, the on-line savings bank (from Prudential) who offered higher rates of interest than terrestrial banks could because of their lower underlying costs. Egg soon found out, however, that they were not alone, for within a couple of months, If (from the Halifax) and Cahoot (Abbey National) were there too and so Egg's competitive edge within the savings market had been lost. What the City euphemistically calls 'adjustments' were made in both the perception of the value of Egg and the positioning of the other on-line offerings juxtaposed against one another.

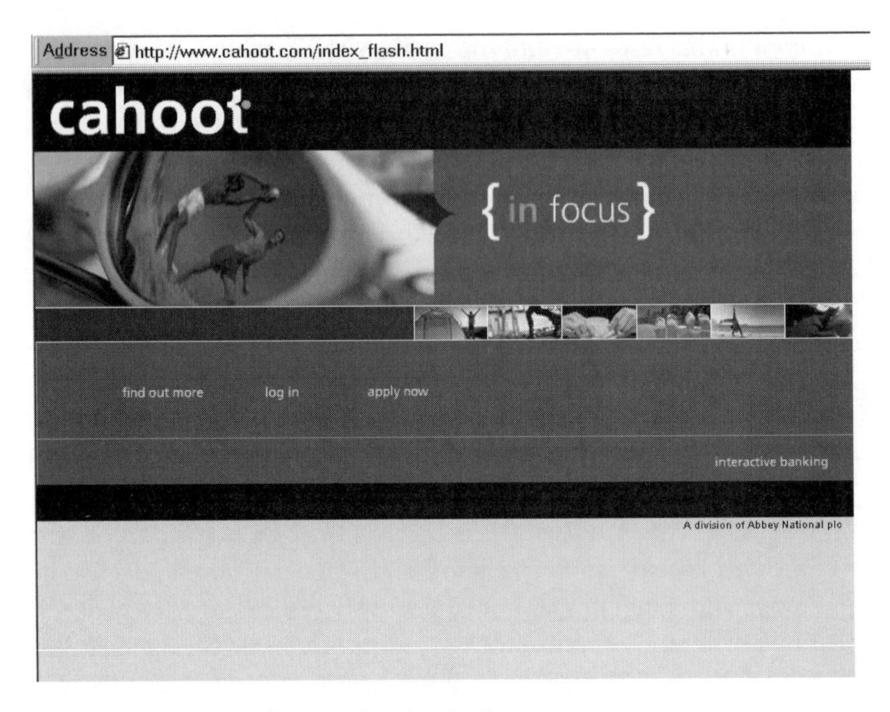

Fig. 5.3 Cahoot – a reflection of on-line banking

Transition stats Barclays find that cross-selling of products has risen, with an average of 2.7 products per client for on-line clients (*Financial Times*, August 2000). This statistic is as good as those found in selling insurance products face to face.

Let's put this all into perspective by quoting Nicholas Crafts of the London School of Economics: 'The Internet is not unprecedented but we might be talking about an extra 0.5 per cent a year on productivity growth, which is about what we saw in those earlier revolutions [railways, telephone and electrification].'

The Internet has been responsible for some wild and woolly thoughts – and some wild and woolly plans too. When a business goes for an IPO it needs money – or it wouldn't bother going for the IPO in the first place.

The new Internet entrepreneurs had ambitious plans to float and become millionaires before the age of 30, and the IPO became a badge – a status symbol – to show that you had joined that exclusive ethereal band, the inner group of Net entrepreneurs. The route to IPO is littered with misunderstood ideas and even more misunderstood opportunities. This points to a communications gap between investors and entrepreneurs as well as a knowledge gap.

US investors have always been happier to take risks and encourage entrepreneurs than those over on this side of the pond. Valuing an Internet company is bound to cause trouble because of the lack of assets – well, assets that can be realised if the company were to founder on the rocks. Our traditional high street banks – ever the merchants of two per cent, low-risk, low-return investment – have always taken the stance of looking at every business venture as if it were a *gone* concern rather than a *going* concern. After all, Net ventures are, of necessity, peopled with assets on legs! If you were only thinking of funding a two per cent margin, low-risk venture then you too would find the risk involved in funding a people-and-ether business difficult to justify – however hard you tried.

Back in the late 1970s and early 1980s the same problems arose with software houses. Business start-ups dependent on computer techies, who could walk out if they got fed up, had trouble in getting funding from all but the most enlightened business development managers in the banks' local branch networks. With venture capitalists they fared slightly differently, but the demand for equity was too much of a give-away in most of the entrepreneurs' estimation.

The recent phenomenon of Internet business incubators is interesting. Whilst there have been successful ones operating in the USA, translating the concept into the UK has not been without its pitfalls. These incubators work on the principle of reducing the risk for the investors (as well as the entrepreneurs) by providing office space and facilities, skills, mentoring – in fact all the things that entrepreneurs usually lack – as well as the funding. For instance there is undoubtedly a lower failure rate for businesses that have been incubated in Fairfax County, south of Washington DC, where eight out of ten businesses treated in this way succeed. In the normal funding and go-it-alone route one in three fail.

The attitude to funding and risk is very different between the USA and the UK – even with new initiatives arriving daily. In the UK there is a rather grudging approach to handing out funding and then, assuming that the funding job is done, the funders disappear over the horizon to let the business grow or fail. Months later they'll reappear to ask how things are going.

There is also a huge battle to get the right sums allocated. For instance, if the business plan identifies that you will need, say, £3 million, you will probably find that the venture capitalists will assume you have over-allowed in the plan and so you will only be offered £1 million. In the USA, on the other hand, it'll be more likely that the same plan requesting three million will be offered seven million or even ten million and the funders look after you on a day-to-day basis too! You'll get the support as well as the money you really do need.

The Net has skewed the business models around once again – making it more difficult to relate current plans to the tried-and-tested business models. Internet entrepreneurs place an emphasis on building critical mass and branding, whether it be in a community-based business or in a fully Internet-enabled e-commerce business. Long-term investments needed to fulfil some business plans are often simply not understood by either the investors or the entrepreneurs and so some investors have jumped ship prematurely and some have simply seen the errors in the pioneers' business models and then pulled the plug.

Pioneers always suffer for being first, but they can also gain the glory and the branding of being out there in front – whether they ultimately succeed or fail.

6

INTREPID PIONEERS

For very many months now it has been impossible to open up a newspaper and *not* read something about dot com shares and their turbulent rises and falls. Around the turn of the millennium some of those dot coms had started to go sour in the minds of investors and, far from being the darlings of the new economy, they were suddenly taking on the mantle of stock market pariahs – companies to be avoided at all costs by savvy investors.

The grand-daddy of them all, Amazon, is probably the most quoted of all Internet-related businesses. Its founder (or chief meddler, as he describes himself) Jeff Bezos spent hundreds of millions of dollars setting up his global empire, with a strategy focused on exploiting his first-to-market advantage through aggressive marketing and prominent advertisements. But many an investor has been asking for some time, when will Amazon turn a profit and actually trade in the black?

> **Foundations** The group, founded in 1995, was called Amazon because 'it is the Earth's biggest river and we have the Earth's biggest selection of books'.

In June 2000 a report by Lehman Brothers castigated the on-line retailer for poor inventory management and excessive debt, and argued that Amazon's operating cashflow would actually *worsen* the more it sold. The final screw in the report warned that Amazon

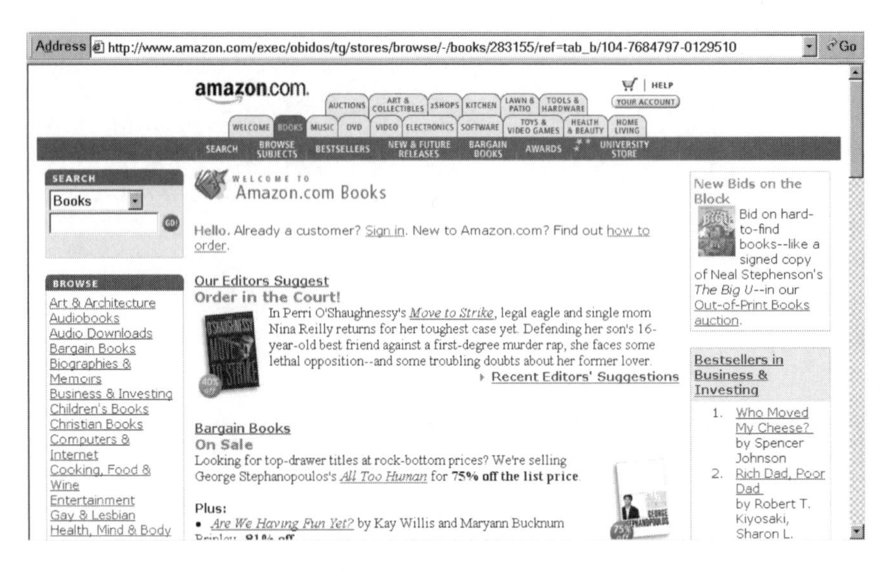

Fig. 6.1 Amazon – the Big Daddy of the book stores

risked running out of cash altogether within a year – and the effect was an immediate meltdown of share prices across Nasdaq with millions of dollars being wiped off Amazon's share price alone.

> **Transition stats** By the middle of 2000, Amazon had seen its share price rising to the dizzy heights of $100, only to see it fall back again to around $40. In one day alone, its shares fell by 20 per cent.

Predictably Jeff Bezos fought back, dismissing the report as 'nonsense', 'baloney' and 'simply wrong'. In a typical example of laid-back pragmatism he told *Sunday Business*: 'We have seen it many times before. Amazon.com has been called Amazon.con, Amazon.toast and Amazon.bomb and my own personal favourite over the years, Amazon.org – because clearly we are a not-for-profit company!'

Initially Amazon targeted the book market, offering substantial discounts on what you would have had to pay in the high street. By being able to hold such a large choice of books, by providing navigation software that not only allowed its customers to find books quickly and easily but also by adding extras such as book reviews and related services, Amazon soon became the preferred choice for people buying books on-line.

> **Whoops!** 'Impersonating authors in Amazon's 'reviews' section is easy, because anyone can submit a review purporting to be written by an author' (the *Independent*, August 2000).

Books were followed by compact discs, electronics, software, home-improvement products and auctions. It also opened up so-called Z-shops whereby other merchants could offer their own products via Amazon's shop front.

Throughout the whole Amazon shopping experience, both brand-building and delivery of sales has been at the forefront of Bezos' way of thinking. As he explained:

> When you first hear about Amazon from a friend, that is part of the customer experience. All the way to when you receive a package, how easy it is to open, and everything in between – is the web site easy to use, one-click shopping, browsing facilities – all those things. All were incorporated to make it easy to use, no matter what you do, to find the thing you're looking for and be able to purchase it quickly and easily without hassle. That sort of minute focus on customer experience is the reason why we have been so successful.

Certainly the Amazon brand is currently unassailable, but whether Amazon continues to be 'successful' and actually head into the black remains to be seen. Yet by any yardstick, Jeff Bezos has become a wealthy man.

Back in the early heady days of e-commerce, many a dot-com entrepreneur had seen their Internet businesses make them an instant fortune – on paper at least.

> **Who'd have thought it** Colin Robinson, the winner of a show on Channel 4 television (which offered £2 million of venture capital as prize money for an original Internet idea), sold his business for shares that could be worth as much as £7 million just three days after picking up his award.

One dot-com millionairess, Martha Lane-Fox, shot to fame with the rise, fall and resurrection of the now infamous Lastminute.com. After its flotation in the spring of 2000, which was massively over subscribed, Lastminute suddenly hit troubled waters as investors started (a bit late in the day, many would argue) to query where all the revenue would come from. (Even the *Financial Times*' 'Lex' column had, prior to flotation, warned of the risks of investing in the business.)

Who'd have thought it? Such is the preoccupation with all things Lastminute.com that a statement from Martha Lane-Fox to 'put the record straight' categorically denying that she was dating actor Neil Morrisey was even reported in the *Daily Telegraph*.

Fig. 6.2 Instant gratification from Lastminute

Analysts predicted after its first six months' trading that it was unlikely to report a pre-tax profit until 2004, with first-year losses likely to be in the order of £30 million. But Martha Lane-Fox remains highly optimistic, pointing out that we are just at the beginning of what will be a hugely profitable global industry. She cited a speech she had heard given by Masayoshi Son, the founder of Softbank Inc., one of the world's biggest Internet investors.

He had begun by asking his audience to raise their hands if they thought the companies selling to consumers over the Web were overvalued. The whole audience threw their hands in the air. 'Aha!' he cried. 'Now who thinks that the Internet consumer sector will be more valuable than the personal computer sector?' Again the whole audience raised its hands. 'Interesting anomaly,' said Son. 'Currently the Internet sector is valued at $1 trillion and the PC sector at $6 trillion.'

Continuing her theme, Martha Lane-Fox points out that most consumer websites are growing in size by 30 per cent every three months – the fastest growth rates of any industry in history. She maintains:

> Investors should be buying shares for the future, not to make a quick buck. The Internet industry is only now at the beginning of its lifetime and I do not believe we have even started to tap into the value that the winning companies in the sector will create.

Despite her obvious enthusiasm, however, others remain highly sceptical. Justin Urquhart Stewart, of Barclays Stockbrokers, told the *Sunday Times* (2 July 2000) that in his view 'dot coms are basically on-line shops and should not be confused with some of the genuine high-tech companies with business-to-business models,' adding that 'for the time being, I would keep my wallet shut and not be tempted to invest in something that is very likely to be dot gone.'

One of the 'dot gones' that Urquhart Stewart must have had at the back of his mind was the very public collapse of the sports e-tailer Boo.com in May 2000, which lost huge amounts for its investors. Here was a very high-profile company that spent, literally, a fortune on its advertising and branding, but which – ultimately – was unable to deliver on its promise of customer friendliness and ease of use. Many argued that it presented a tricky path to the goods on offer and was 'too clever by half' in the technology it used.

As one disgruntled reader wrote in an Internet magazine, 'I doubt that Boo's managers were able to track their sales and revenues on the back of a fag packet, and in that fact lies their demise' (the *Industry Standard*, March 2000).

As many a 'dot gone' company has now learned – and is still learning – success, both off-line and on-line, will always go to companies that follow time-honoured business principles: plan carefully, ensure you can deliver to your customers, control and target your marketing and build revenue streams.

A problem, though, also comes when big profile names such as Amazon upset the market, causing a tidal wave to engulf the smaller dot coms that are struggling to stay afloat. Such was one of the excuses given out by the ailing clickmango.com when, in July 2000, it hit stormy waters just three months after its successful and colourful float.

> **Who'd have thought it?** Despite failing to find a possible trade buyer for its website, clickmango.com has nevertheless received an offer for its circular plastic boardroom (*Financial Times*, August 2000).

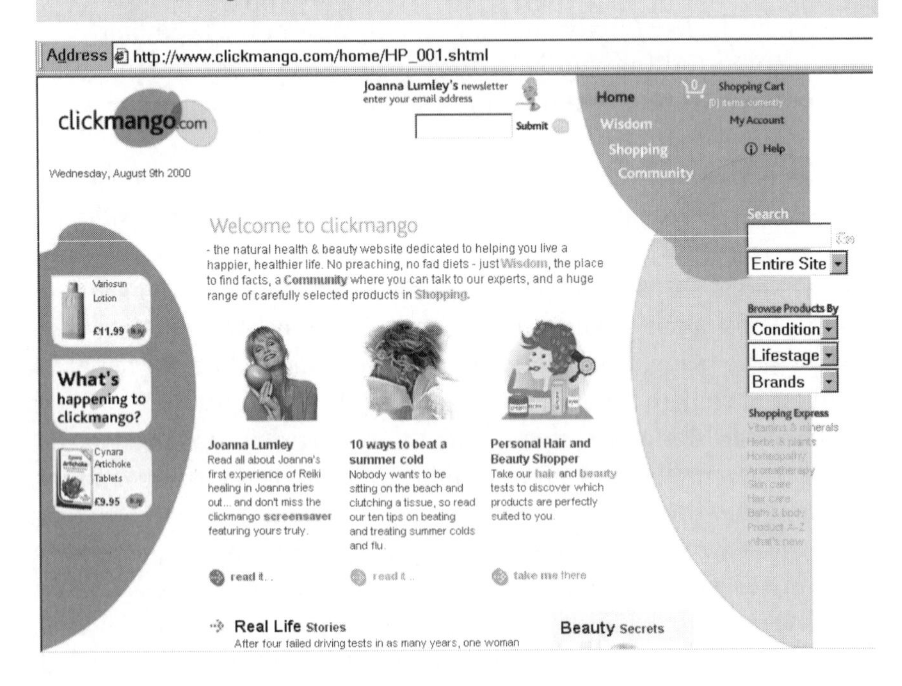

Fig. 6.3 clickmango's absolutely fabulous site

Clickmango – an Internet health and beauty company – set a new record for procuring investment: in September 1999 it raised £3 million from venture capitalists in just eight days. Toby Rowland (son of the late tycoon Tiny Rowland) said that the falling fortunes of Internet giants such as Amazon had made it almost impossible to get more money when they had tried to raise £300, 000 to keep the company going for another three months. 'The sad thing is that it looks as if we will never get the opportunity to see whether this business would have worked,' he said. 'Yet we were under budget and over our sales targets.' So was it just investor cold feet?

Transition stats

A snapshot of private equity investment by sector:

Sector	%
Computer software	32%
Internet technology	17%
Communications, carriers	13%
Biotechnology	9%
Other electronics related	7%
Computer services	6%
Communications hardware	6%
Computer hardware	5%
Medical instruments, devices	3%

(*Source:* PricewaterhouseCoopers, June 2000)

What lessons are there to be learned? Can new Internet start-ups succeed in a world that has now been tainted with such vast numbers of failures? According to the American research firm International Data Corporation (IDC) new ventures need to square up to commercial realities, and can no longer use the excuse that they are new businesses operating in a virgin environment where the rules have yet to be set.

At IDC's annual e-Commerce Forum in Paris, one of its senior vice presidents, Gigi Wang, said that there was a clear difference between dot com thinking at the end of the last century and at the start of the present one:

> The first phase of e-commerce was all about building the infrastructure and getting the eyeballs and stickiness. You didn't look

> at the revenues being generated. In the second phase, we don't expect to see vast numbers of new people coming to the Internet, but we do expect that we have to see a vast upturn in the levels of revenues.

Put another way, Wang said that the lack of what were, after all, commonsense business requirements served only to highlight the fool's paradise in which the entire dot com industry had been living for the past few years. 'One of the characteristics of the survivor companies,' she said, 'is that they have all had someone with solid business experience. You don't put a 20-year-old with long hair in charge of the company.'

The delegates were told that there would be a clear need to show a healthy income statement with, at the very least, a solid strategy in place for when the company could genuinely expect to make it into the black.

Unfortunately, the omens do not look good – at least in the short term. In one of its regular polls of 600 company executives who have responsibility for their firms' on-line strategies, IDC found that a staggering 34 per cent either did not know when, if ever, they were likely to become profitable or claimed to have no method of evaluating their profitability!

In this new era of Internet enlightenment, can anyone really expect these firms to be in business in a few years' time? The path to wealth and longevity is littered with the banana skins of ignorance and lack of planning.

7

STARTING BLOCKS

The advent of the Internet offers the perfect opportunity for reviewing a company, its products, its core business and its relationships with its customers and suppliers.

Before you go spending megabucks, any change in the way your business works should be looked at holistically – otherwise you could find that there are considerable glitches that are likely to occur before you have made contingency plans for them. Hiccups like that can be avoided and the risks of developing a new venture or a new way of working can be reduced substantially.

Transition info Millions have been frittered away by big companies trying to create Internet operations (*Financial Times*, August 2000).

In much the same way as you would review accounting, HR or communications within your company, you can review Internet awareness and usage and the impact it could have on your business.

The purpose of an accounting audit is to gain a snapshot of the company at any given time and show where the assets and liabilities are. The same philosophy applies to e-commerce and Internet technologies – to let you see the wood for the trees and appraise the current state of the Internet within your company. Then you can get on with planning the next phase, having identified what other assets, skills and education you may need to acquire – along with setting up intranets and extranets, and ensuring that your Internet presence is up to speed. We call this whole process an Internet audit.

In the UK the Internet Audit Company (IAC) was set up in 1999 to address this particular need and has created benchmarks for assessment on a valuation/liability level, as well as on the practical level of skills, awareness and current usage (compared with those aspired to and needed to achieve the levels of usage required by the business). Having completed an audit, you can then position a company correctly and devise a route map for the foreseeable future so that your vision can be realistically achieved.

As the Internet and wireless technologies sweep relentlessly through industry and the way we all live, it should be normal practice for a company's websites and Internet technology usage to be reviewed regularly. Keeping an eye on the long-term objectives is essential if the short-term milestones are to lead to anywhere meaningfully and profitably for the business. The Internet and wireless technologies are becoming such powerful and important media and distribution channels that any business ignores them at its peril. Because of the fast rate of change in these relatively new media it is all the more likely that short-term goals will be addressed without devoting enough strategic planning of the long term.

The purpose of an audit is to find out what the organisation wants and needs from its current and future Web presence, both internally and externally, so that a positioning paper (which is essentially a business plan) can be prepared. In this, the relationships between the different departments, their target markets and their objectives have all to be considered. There may well be areas where those objectives differ and clash with one another, but the overall benefit to the firm needs to be paramount to any benefits to individual departments.

The websites should, of course, work well for all these departments. Consideration needs to be given as to what your key messages are, how the messages are being put across, who your key target audiences are and, not least, what the potential visitors will make of the sites. The normal synergy between the different departments in a company needs to be reflected on the Web so that one reinforces the messages from another without apparent fragmentation of the business as viewed by outsiders. The latter is often the case if a proper planning process has not been gone through.

IAC, which was set up by seasoned business people who are also Internet cognoscenti, has also devised a benchmarking tool to assess websites from a variety of perspectives. Using this can help a business to focus its messages toward the target markets.

A properly conducted audit should define precisely what the organisation has achieved (and not achieved) with its websites as they currently stand, as well as the use of Internet technologies inside and outside the business. Only then will it identify the plans, aspirations and targets of each department and key players, look at how the company can gain exponentially from its Web presence and consider any future development into other Internet involvements.

There are likely to be a number of missed Internet opportunities that sooner or later the business will have to come to grips with. All too often plans are drawn up for marketing materials, websites, or even business processes without identifying the areas that really need to be thought through. These plans produce a 'sticking plaster' type of review that may well hold good for a couple of months but works against the company in the longer term.

There are also benefits to the company if the key players all 'own' their input to the audit. The adoption and implementation of the strategy and detail identified in the positioning paper will ensure that the team is all behind the arrowhead since their concerns, hopes and aspirations for the site and the company will have been expressed.

Any website needs to have a good business reason for its very existence. There are many websites that appear to meander about, rather than having a quiet confidence and easy navigation path. The Web is a positive genre. You cannot be a 'nothing' on the Web or else you will be ignored – and that should definitely not be an option for any company.

Sites currently up on the Web need to be rethought regularly in order to meet the demands of the Internet visitor – from whichever target market they may originate. Some key target audiences may well be being overlooked, and there may well be other areas of content and usability that need to be addressed.

The audit will identify your target audiences and the messages you want to put across to each one, and assess where one department can reinforce the messages from another (and similarly where a message can appear to be at odds with another).

A positioning paper can then consider the opportunities for e-commerce and other key areas where a Web presence, or revised Web presence, and further use of Internet technologies could dramatically enhance the business. Accurate information on the impact of this enhancement permeating through the different business processes employed (together with costings, additional and alternative methodologies, their learning curves and their required IT and technological infrastructure) can be factored in.

Naturally, part of the process will involve a long critical look at your current Internet presence, with recommendations of where certain aspects of it need tightening up or refocusing.

The positioning paper will identify key skills shortages amongst your staff, and suggest ways of circumventing such shortages. It should cover the issue of bringing in different Web aspects under one roof (if that is appropriate) and aid the drawing of a route map of how that could be best achieved. Criteria for the recruitment and selection of specialist key staff could be drawn up, including many of the technical aspects that would need to be considered.

From the positioning paper a flexible route map will enable scheduling of all necessary changes, training, purchases, implementations and subsequent testing of procedures. The most difficult thing of all is to change the mindsets of the individuals within the company and the adoption of any new angle to the established corporate mindset.

> **Who'd have thought it?** During the first day of a full Internet audit conducted by IAC for a small media company, savings of £30,000 p.a. were identified in one small area alone.

Obviously it is easier for an outside company to come in and conduct an Internet audit than it is for you to do it yourself. Fresh eyes on the business, together with interviews of key people by experts who have no internal political axes to grind, ensure a clearer and more complete picture of the realities, without the oft-found protectionist groupings and communications constipation created by middle management.

Most Internet audits identify areas where large annual savings can be made by the streamlining of process. Within business, as in life in general, processes and habits grow organically and the opportunity to reappraise the purpose as well as the form and function of your business – together with the implementation of higher grade technology – is a perfect time for change without enormous threat to individuals.

Basic areas covered by IAC are:

- *Summary and urgent actions*
  There are a number of splendid opportunities and serious threats that are likely to affect the strategy and the subsequent business plan for the whole of the business. These will need to be addressed urgently as they are at the very heart of the way that companies will perform in the future. Because of the speed of change in Internet technology, and the resultant take-up within businesses of the opportunities offered, time is of the essence in considering, implementing and launching an Internet-based strategic plan, or an extended Internet-based strategic plan and route map for your business.

- *Board meeting*
  The proposals should always be debated at board level and certainly not just left to technically able people. A quantum shift in the business's position may well be necessary. The change in distribution channels has the propensity to change everything. Parts of the business may well face annihilation in the next few years if the threats are not addressed and opportunities not taken. Repositioning the company in the marketplace is the only way to take advantage of the new climate created by these changes.

- *Websites*
  Existing websites may well need urgent review if the company is to be taken seriously in Internet and business terms. All websites should be constructed with a view to building up massive and comprehensive databases of potential prospects – all properly qualified and therefore of great commercial value.

Site lines Check out your website free of charge at **www.e-biz-pro.org**, **www.Internetauditcompany.com** or **www.topspin-group.com** for an instant picture of how your site is driving.

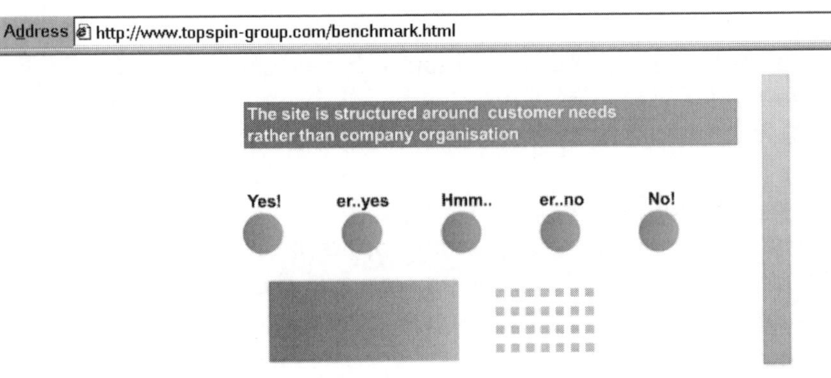

Fig. 7.1 Check how your site is driving

- *Branding*
  All branding implications will need to be reviewed, including domain names and the impact they have on your brand.

- *E-mail*
  A comprehensive e-mail policy across the company needs to be reviewed, agreed and implemented without delay.

- *Intranet – knowledge management and internal communications*
  The board should consider the setting up of an intranet/extranet or the extension of same, with a phased implementation plan in order to enhance knowledge management and internal communications. The chief executive and senior management should, at the very least, be able to access accounts, sales figures etc. as well as other pertinent information when travelling. The demand for access to the business's central information systems from remote working will increase as the activities of the business diversify and globalise. Good foundations, in the form of a well thought out, but easily operated, intranet will prove their worth within months.

> **Who'd have thought it?** Most well planned corporate intranets pay for themselves within three to six months of their implementation.

- *Investor and city*
  If it has not already been done, provision should be made for automating the system of supplying information to investors and

analysts. In addition, adequate background information on the company and its up-to-date activities should be available on the website, making it a source to which telephone and other enquiries can be directed.

- *Merger or acquisition*
  Consideration must be given to merger, alliance or acquisition of an e-commerce big name – or buying time on one in order to achieve pole position.

- *IT skills*
  An urgent review of IT and skills sets needs to be carried out within the whole company.

- *Extranet*
  Suppliers and partners need to be given passworded access to the company's extranet in order to improve information and cashflow. This goes hand in hand with developing closer relationships with those on whom the business depends.

- *Remote working*
  A travelling person given a heavy laptop cannot travel light. It is also more difficult to train someone who is travelling a lot. Another danger of remote working is that required mindset changes may also be more difficult to achieve because of the lack of exposure to the day-to-day changes in corporate culture.

- *Training*
  Throughout the business a number of people are likely to identify that they need some training in order to use their equipment effectively. As more systems are implemented these training needs must be factored in for the office to function properly. This could take the form of personal training, as well as help files and suggestions placed on the intranet.

So where to go from here? The solution is clear. Take a look at the rules that apply to e-commerce and business that you'll find in the next chapter and call in your Internet auditors so that you are on a firm foundation before you write your route map. Remember that the percentage of revenues coming from e-business today is about 9.8 per cent, whilst by 2003 it will be nearer 21 per cent and by 2006 more like 39 per cent.

8

E-COMMERCE RULES – SOME OF THEM GOLDEN OLDIES

Having bought a book entitled *E-commerce without tears* you would expect to be able to glean a whole load of useful information on the golden rules you should apply to your on-line venture. Well, to save you the trouble of scrabbling madly through this tome, we've lumped all the golden rules together into this chapter.

It has to be said that some of these rules are plain common sense, but others appear at first glance to fly in the face of what you might have picked up from the accepted wisdom of traditional businesses.

OUTSOURCE YOUR BUSINESS PROCESSES TO YOUR CUSTOMERS

Can you remember way back when, when the giant supermarket chains were anything but giants? Sainsbury's, for instance, started off as a simple grocer's shop over a century ago and gradually increased its number of outlets. Customer service meant patting a wedge of butter to exactly 5 oz or slicing a salami to a specific thickness.

Then the concept of supermarkets crossed the Atlantic and we Brits finally woke up to a great new concept. Why pay staff to gather individual items from the shop shelves when your customers would be perfectly happy to do the same thing themselves for free?

Garages soon got in on the act. Why pay staff to pump petrol when the motorists would be just as willing to do the job themselves?

The do-it-yourself concept of customer service appears to be a cultural thing. In Saudi Arabia, for instance, supermarkets are to be found in all the main shopping arcades; but drive to a garage and it would be unthinkable for you to get out and get your hands dirty by filling up your car. Perhaps it is something to do with the fact that petrol is cheaper than water; or more likely that the use of servants – not to mention the fact that everyone fits into a social hierarchy – is deeply embedded within society.

This simple idea has even been publicly eschewed by the high street banks. Barclays, for instance, had a TV advertisement proclaiming the benefits of being able to pay bills and transfer money on-line. It featured one of its customers, in the form of Robbie Coltrane, declaring 'So we're all going to be bank managers now are we?'

Of course, the banks had already implemented this concept back in the 1980s when they started using ATMs – or hole-in-the-wall machines. By automating the process, the banks were able to free up their staff for 'other duties' (or 'downsize' to reduce their costs) and the customer was spared the hassle of having to get to a bank during opening hours – and often waiting in a longer queue!

The Internet can also allow you to outsource to your customers – a.k.a. get your customers to do all the work and charge them for the privilege! How many commercial websites don't now feature information about products and services, tutorials or general help, in order to free up the time of the employees and also give customers access to the information 24 hours a day?

E-commerce allows much more, though, than instant access to information. The heart of most e-commerce websites lies in the implementation of on-line ordering, on-line payment systems and – in some cases – even on-line delivery of services or products.

CUT YOUR COSTS OF DISTRIBUTION, EVEN IF IT HURTS YOUR PRESENT BUSINESS

This is a difficult concept for many businesses to understand, let alone put into practice. Hurting your present business in order to get your e-business off the ground appears to be folly to most people.

The problem is that if you don't face the unpalatable truth now, it could be that your business will pay the price in months to come. Take the area of book sales, for instance. We all know that the sale of books and CDs on the Internet has captured the lion's share of e-commerce-enabled websites. What the likes of Amazon and Alphabet Street discovered was that by cutting out the middle men and selling directly to the end user, they could slash their costs dramatically.

So what of Waterstone's and Dillons and all the other brand-name book stores that now had to square up to the fact that with the new Internet interlopers threatening their core business, they also had to have an on-line presence? The problem was that if they wanted to compete effectively with Amazon they would need to reduce the cover prices by around 20 per cent. But then what should they charge their bricks-and-mortar store customers who would be confused by a

Fig. 8.1 Waterstone's are still big in the high street

dual pricing structure if they charged higher prices on the high street than they did on their websites?

The jury is still out on this issue as many book buyers like to browse the shelves before they make their decision; but the fact is that Amazon changed the art of bookselling almost overnight, and it will never be the same again.

The trick, then, is to educate your customers to use the Internet route to purchasing wherever possible, rather than using the bricks-and-mortar stores. That way as one model (the physical stores) fades away, a new model (the e-commerce site) comes to the fore.

Ignore this golden rule at your peril. E-commerce adds sharks to the ocean of transactions and it is a real example of eat or be eaten. If you hedge your bets by attempting to cannibalise only areas of the market in which you are not active, then the likelihood is that someone else will come along and steal your entire market from under your nose – and you won't be able to do a thing about it!

The problem is that businesses see all that they have invested in a company and fear losing it or worse, upsetting the shareholders. The implication is that you should make the investment in the new operation and throw away the old model if it can't compete. If you are really good, you will make both concepts succeed, but it is a frightening thing for any business to contemplate, especially if it has been doing very well up to now.

TREAT EACH CUSTOMER AS AN INDIVIDUAL

A century ago the would-be car buyer looking for a smart new Model T was told categorically 'You can have any colour you like – just so long as it is black.' In today's modern world customers not only want, but expect, to get whatever they want. Henry Ford's view of the world just won't wash any more.

And the concept of getting what you want applies with extra vigour to the Web. News sites, for instance, can supply news personalised for their readers. This can be done in a number of ways. For instance, when signing up to receive pages a visitor arriving at the site might be asked to tick a number of boxes regarding subjects in which they have an interest. Subsequently, pages can be dynamically generated highlighting these stories specifically reflecting those choices.

Newer sites use 'intelligent' software that records the types of pages visitors have visited and then ranks its output according to his previously viewed content. Often it uses 'cookies' stored in the system folder on the visitors' computers to identify them when they return for a second visit.

Apart from generating news stories 'on the fly', this concept can usefully be extended to the sale of physical products such as books. Nowadays, whenever you log on to a book site, the chances are that whatever you enter into the site's search engine will generate advertisements on the Web page pertinent to your query.

This technique is akin to a well-used marketing technique known as 'niching', which involves breaking down customers individually by traits and rebuilding them into unique groups called 'communities of value'.

The truth is, though, that if you haven't started to treat your present customers as individuals anyway, your business will have been losing out already.

CREATE COMMUNITIES OF VALUE

This is the second part of the niching concept we just talked about. After customers have been identified by individual traits, they are recombined into customer groups. What we're aiming at is to supply helpful information within an environment where like-minded individuals can get together and later be mobilised to purchase products.

Specific product-related sites cater for these like-minded communities and draw them in by the comfort factor of having their particular need, fetish or hobby given all the help, information and resources they could possibly want. In such an environment your marketing messages are much more likely to find a ready audience and sales of your product or service should thereby increase.

RETHINK THE INTERACTION WITH YOUR CUSTOMERS

In the last 50 years customer service has taken a right old bashing. Not only is it considered 'normal' to have to contend with rude shop assistants who would rather gossip with one another than offer you any service, but the dreadful organisation of many call centres – whose sole purpose seems to be to save their parent organisations money – leaves many of their customers, whom they should be trying to woo, vowing that they never want to deal with them again. This seems to be a British disease and is in stark contrast to the 'have a nice day' experience so widely adopted in the USA.

Let's face it. If you had the choice of dealing with the vagaries of a customer service centre over the phone – where you are constantly passed from one 'customer care assistant' to another whilst being wooed with a dreadful music tape loop – or being allowed to sort your problem out over a website, which would you choose?

We know our answer only too well, having experienced the 'service' meted out by many call centres over a number of months this past year.

The problem with many of them is that they start off their call centre operations with one question at the forefront of their minds. How can we save money by automating as much as possible? Rather than aiming to woo their customers by asking, 'What can we do to automate the process and make life easier for our customers?'

So when you ring up a help desk and find yourself having to go through the rigmarole of pressing '*' to identify that you have a keypad phone, followed by '1', '2', '3' or '4', depending on which department you wish to connect to, followed by '1', '2', '3' or '4', depending on which service you require and when you finally get to speak to one of the assistants you very quickly find out that they only have the answers to a small number of questions so invariably you then have to be passed on to someone else – often at the other end of the country – who might just know the answer.

Sounds familiar? There are all too many service companies who treat their customers in this dreadful way.

And then they compound the problem – of their own making – by assuming that they know what their customers think without asking them! (If you don't believe us, try ringing some of them 'out-of-hours' with a query, but don't be surprised to discover that they know full well – even if the rest of the world disagrees – that all businesses stop work for the day at 5.00 pm and totally close at weekends!)

One e-commerce firm we once worked with had a similar attitude to its customers, whereby it 'knew' what the customers wanted even though it had never stopped to ask them. It was only when a new MD was brought in that the rot was stopped and the firm started to learn what customer service was really all about and that the products, as currently packaged, were *not* what the customers wanted! This wasn't because the old MD was arrogant; it was because he found some of the technical stuff straightforward and he simply assumed that all his customers would be able to cope with the demands of his Web service in a similar way. (For this reason alone you should make sure that your techies – computer or otherwise – don't rule your Web presence.)

So, wherever possible, provide an electronic interface for your customers. That way, your organisation can maintain complete control over the interface and not only capture information, but also instantaneously provide better responses by using this information to learn and memorise. In addition, websites don't (normally) have 'bad hair days'!

A little suggestion for you: whatever the state of your website, be it e-commerce-enabled or not, why not position a customer feedback box to let the customers tell you exactly what they think of your site and your company? It may make unpalatable reading (although we hope not) but just think how much valuable information you will get to help you with your product and service development, as well as your marketing, and all for very little cost – and perhaps a few red faces.

PUT THE CUSTOMERS' EASE OF USE OVER AND ABOVE THAT OF YOUR OWN

As long as there is familiarity, customers will use your company's new technology instead of a competitor's. The temptation amongst companies, however, is to stick to what they are used to. That's perfectly natural. People avoid change when they can.

But the Internet changes all the rules, so if you're going to have to adapt, why not take the opportunity to provide that little something extra for your customers?

Take the big courier companies, for example. DHL, Fedex, UPS and TNT are just four examples of couriers that let you track the progress of your shipment to its destination. By connecting their websites to their back-end systems (which have to track the progress of parcels anyway) these companies offer a facility that is truly appreciated by their customers and get them coming back again and again. These companies save themselves tremendous amounts of money by making their tracking system transparent to their customers – and save themselves irate communications in the process.

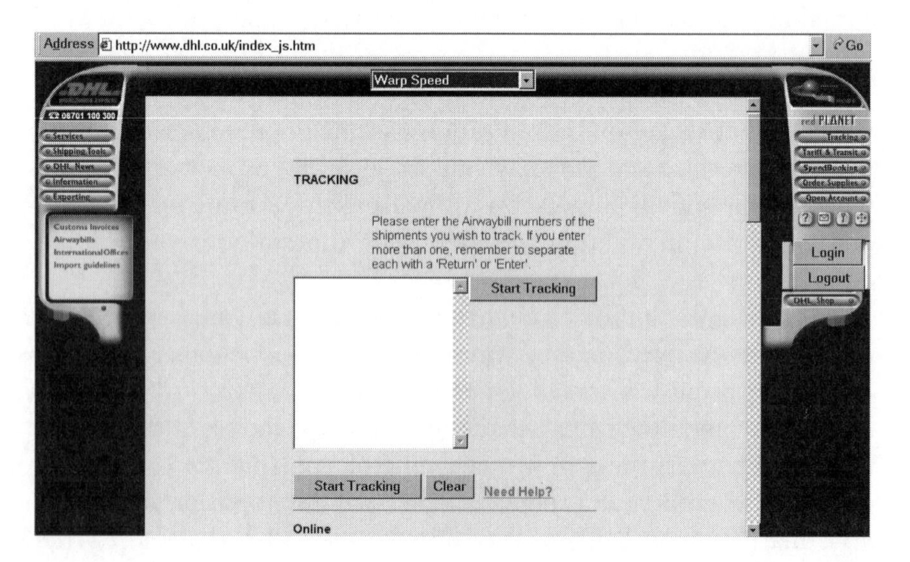

Fig. 8.2 DHL's self-drive customer service – at warp speed

In addition, by using data mining techniques (see Chapter 19) other processes can be automated to your customers' requirements and you'll end up with a site that provides much more value.

GIVE AWAY AS MUCH AS YOU POSSIBLY CAN

Information is relatively free and widely available. If you hold on to information, thinking that it provides you with a competitive advantage, then think again. There are a number of companies that 'missed the boat' when the Internet grew in popularity, because they treated their internal information as an asset that would provide a greater return. This even includes the specifications or standards for their products.

But nothing is secret, and the first casualties of the new information order were the companies that failed to gain a 'first-to-market' advantage by enticing customers with free information. You can now get free information everywhere, and customers will always gravitate toward free information, products, or services and away from proprietary or fee-based information services. They will even pay in other more subtle ways for this content, and since they attach a value to information, that is what attracts them to a website.

If enough customers can be attracted, then concepts such as critical mass and creating communities of value will start to have a significant impact on the market value of the organisation supplying the information.

But what's in it for you if you give everything away for free? Well, consider two companies; one that provides information over the Net for a subscription and one that provides it for free. The pay-per-view company signs up some customers and immediately has the resources to edit and write data. The free company, on the other hand, adds a way for visitors to post their own information.

It is clear that visitors to company A will be limited but profitable, while visitors to company B will be vast but non-paying. But what if you called a company in a related product field and asked them if they wanted to advertise on your site? You tell them that a vast number of customers come to your site for free information.

Eventually, the growth in company B's website could eclipse that of the paid-for website, with the eventual total demise of the latter. The moral is clear: give the information away for free and capitalise on the other benefits of critical mass.

Now, we're not suggesting for one moment that you should go to the extraordinary lengths of giving everything away for free, such as when Barclays inadvertently allowed anyone to access anyone else's on-line account by having inadequate security in place. (Since the advent of the Internet, would it have been better to take a different approach? What we have seen so far could be just the tip of the iceberg. If people lose faith in the banks, history has shown that they withdraw all their money. It could lead to a run on the banks. The unscrupulous could have had enough time to get their organised act together and set up the necessary procedures to cause Barclays customers huge problems.)

> **Whoops!** Security scares about Barclays have drawn the comment from Matt Barrett, Chief Executive of Barclays, that the glitch 'had been unacceptable and the bank was working flat out to fix it' (*Financial Times*, August 2000).

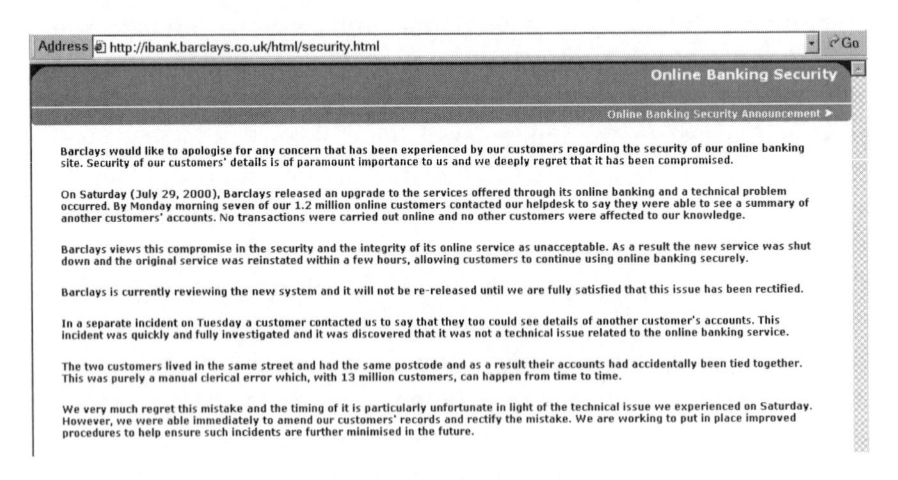

Address http://ibank.barclays.co.uk/html/security.html

Online Banking Security

Online Banking Security Announcement

Barclays would like to apologise for any concern that has been experienced by our customers regarding the security of our online banking site. Security of our customers' details is of paramount importance to us and we deeply regret that it has been compromised.

On Saturday (July 29, 2000), Barclays released an upgrade to the services offered through its online banking and a technical problem occurred. By Monday morning seven of our 1.2 million online customers contacted our helpdesk to say they were able to see a summary of another customers' accounts. No transactions were carried out online and no other customers were affected to our knowledge.

Barclays views this compromise in the security and the integrity of its online service as unacceptable. As a result the new service was shut down and the original service was reinstated within a few hours, allowing customers to continue using online banking securely.

Barclays is currently reviewing the new system and it will not be re-released until we are fully satisfied that this issue has been rectified.

In a separate incident on Tuesday a customer contacted us to say that they too could see details of another customer's accounts. This incident was quickly and fully investigated and it was discovered that it was not a technical issue related to the online banking service.

The two customers lived in the same street and had the same postcode and as a result their accounts had accidentally been tied together. This was purely a manual clerical error which, with 13 million customers, can happen from time to time.

We very much regret this mistake and the timing of it is particularly unfortunate in light of the technical issue we experienced on Saturday. However, we were able immediately to amend our customers' records and rectify the mistake. We are working to put in place improved procedures to help ensure such incidents are further minimised in the future.

Fig. 8.3 Barclays' very public apology

Look instead at the fortunes of the Internet forum *First Tuesday* that gave away as much information as possible, thereby gaining

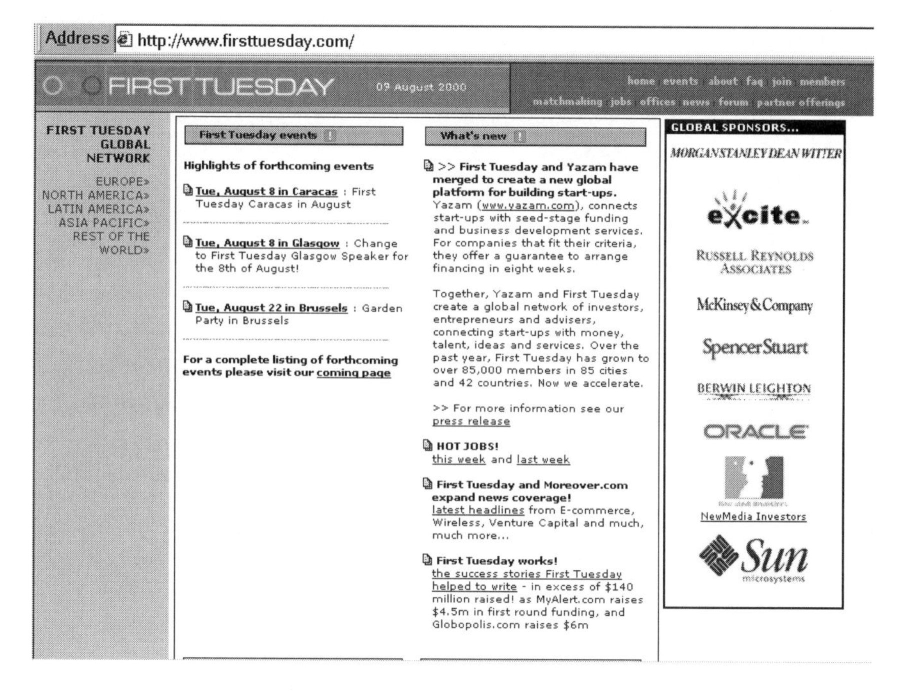

Fig. 8.4 First Tuesday, the prima donna of the schmoozefest

value by attracting huge numbers of visitors to its site. After only 20 months it sold out to the Israeli firm Yazam, which specialises in finding funding for early-stage Internet companies, for around $50 million.

> **Site lines** The principle of giving something away for nothing is amply demonstrated by **www.docta.com** – a site specialising in giving away legal documents. What? Lawyers giving away something for nothing? It seems incredible! Trust us and have a look. You might well be amazed.

STRUCTURE EVERY TRANSACTION AS A JOINT VENTURE

A virtual company, by definition, is a company without infrastructure. So how can it operate? Simply by forming partnerships and

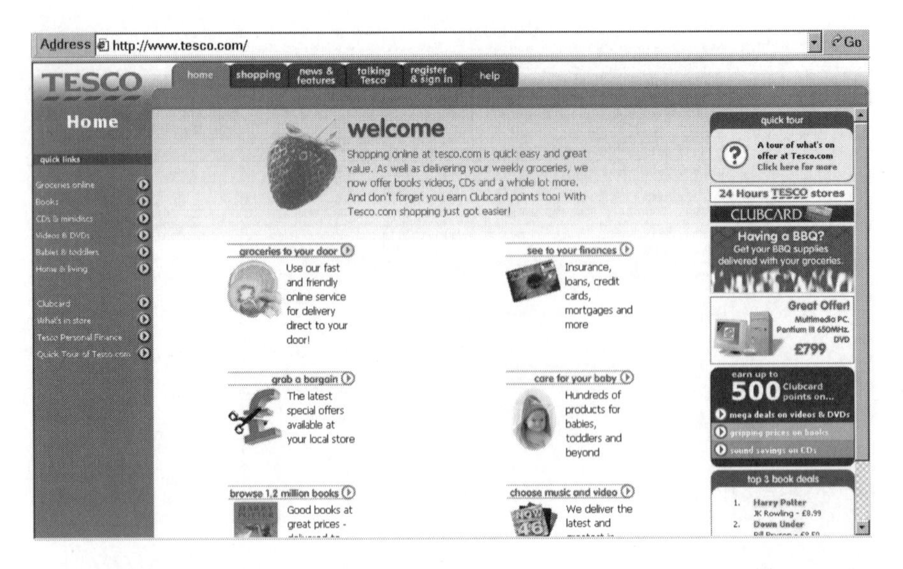

Fig. 8.5 Tesco's wares on display

joint ventures with other organisations that do have some form of structure. But even more importantly, it forms partnerships and joint ventures with its end users.

This concept of joint venturing is now at the point where new companies with no physical structure can compete more effectively than large, older organisations, simply by choosing a series of partners that provide the missing physical structure.

Where would CDNow.com be without distribution companies to wing the recordings to its customers? How would Tesco Direct succeed without having a fleet of vans to deliver its groceries to its end users?

We all remember the near-ubiquitous milk delivery float vans that used to deliver Britain's daily pintas to every doorstep. With the coming of the Internet the dairies have cottoned on to a new business process that could rescue their ailing distribution businesses by allowing them to deliver small-sized Internet-ordered products on their nationwide distribution service.

TREAT YOUR ASSETS AS LIABILITIES

New Internet-based organisations have little in the way of physical assets, which makes them very powerful competition from a financial perspective simply because the return on investment can be astronomical for any revenue. Of course, if your company doesn't own any physical assets, such as land, buildings or plant, there is less pressure to provide a return on that investment. However, with no physical assets you are providing a service only and will therefore be uncompetitive unless you attain brand recognition.

Ideally, asset-based companies should move to an e-commerce model by building or valuing their electronic assets. If they don't, virtual competitors will develop them instead, and the physical, asset-based company will be left on the sidelines as a supplier to a large virtual market with very tight margins.

DO THE UNEXPECTED TO BE ONE STEP AHEAD OF THE COMPETITION

A value chain can be defined as a series of functions that create and distribute an organisation's goods and services. Conducting business in a traditional supply chain model can nowadays be a risky proposition. There are numerous competitors who are after your market share, and they will do their level best to upset the market through the use of new technology.

The concept of destroying your value chain is simple enough: be first to take the risk yourself and upset your competitors, freely giving away value, changing your way of working and cutting out the middlemen, and essentially do what it takes to reposition yourself as the leader of the change process.

Why? Because leaders control the process whilst others are obliged to follow. Leaders can define standards or limit damage. Regardless of what your value chain is, use the power of the digital world and new technology to position your company for the future.

MANAGE INNOVATION AND REAP THE REWARDS

Research and development is expensive, risky and hard to quantify in terms of a projected return on investment or impact on shareholder value. But by diversifying its exposure to new technologies, a company can reap the benefits by being on an inside track to new techniques rather than having to buy in from scratch when the time is right.

The easiest way for a company to participate is to take a small position in many new technologies so that the company is an active participant with relatively low exit costs. Microsoft continually invests in emerging technologies as a minority partner only. That way if the technology fails, its loss is minimal. If the technology succeeds, Microsoft is a participant with an inside track. The key is that any failure is likely to be offset by a successful innovation somewhere else.

TAKE ON THE YOUNGSTERS, BUT DON'T FORGET THE VALUE OF GREY HAIRS

Taking on youngsters does not mean giving teenagers the title of director just to keep them off the streets. But children and young adults have been brought up in a different world from their 40-something parents and the way they interact with technology is totally different from older people; their frame of reference or understanding of technology is also totally different.

Today's young adults have learned by playing computer games that textual information is slow and inefficient, that interfaces should be straightforward to use regardless of what they do, that things should be fun because attention spans are short, and that somewhere out in cyberspace is what they want or need for free.

These concepts are vital to today's business success, and are easily understood by young adults. We would suggest that you simply cannot afford to ignore their insight when planning your killer strategies for your e-commerce site.

But a final word: don't forget the *éminences grises*. We've said it before, but we'll say it again. Businesses of whatever persuasion still need a firm hand on the tiller. Just because you have decided to tear up your traditional business model in favour of Net trading does not mean that you don't need someone who can understand finances, marketing, manufacture ... in fact all the other areas of your business where experience still counts – nay, where it relies – on good old-fashioned experience.

Well, that's got the golden rules out the way, but before you get complacent, turn the page to learn about some of the meteorites floating in the murky depths of cyberspace.

9

ROCKS THAT COULD BLOCK YOUR CYBERSTREAM

DISAPPEARING BUZZ

As the use of the Internet becomes the norm in everyone's mind, the buzz gained from surfing and even from using the Internet will pale. Some usage will reduce as the sexiness of the Net fades and it becomes purely a utility. It was ever thus with innovation.

The collection of information and research will be utilities we all expect to use, utilising personalised e-mail and information gathering, as well as 'push' tools to deliver to customers exactly what they want. Sloppily constructed and maintained sites will lose visitors and business. Likewise, as the Internet becomes more and more a business tool, the joys of playing with it at home will fade. Quicker and easier ways for individuals and companies to gather the information they want from this ultimate utility will, of necessity, mean that communities of value will add value of their own by sifting and refining the information within their area of expertise and making it available for others.

STOP ME IF I'M REPEATING MYSELF

Creating an e-commerce site that will get customers to value it enough to come back again and again is what this business is all about. Whilst the temptation is to build a stunning site and sit back in delight, its whole *raison d'être* is that it should not just stun and amaze visitors but should add value to their visits – each time they visit. It must provide what is called 'repetitive value', for without this your marketing and promotional budget will continue to be huge and your cost of sales will remain high.

The acquisition of critical mass in your customer base is achieved far more efficiently if visitors come back, although you will have to keep promoting your site in order to grow and maintain market share as more and more sites will be vying with you for the same customers. Building loyalty or community is the next part of the plan.

REDUCING VISITOR NUMBERS

Despite the fact that millions of people have still never had access to the Internet, this will change as the price of equipment and the cost of connection to the Internet falls, and high growth rates in Internet traffic are expected in the foreseeable future. With the growth of access channels embracing broadcast and broadband media, as well as mobile telephony, the increase in the numbers of purchases on-line is likely to grow exponentially – as will the number of new websites.

There are millions of websites out there. Most of them receive only a few visitors, relatively speaking; indeed there is a growing group of well known sites that attract the bulk of the Web's visitors. (Don't let anyone persuade you that the numbers of 'hits' reflects the number of visitors to your site. 'Hits' are simply calculated on the basis of the number of images and hyperlinks that are embedded within a particular page. Therefore if a web page has 10 click buttons the number of hits recorded per visitor will be calculated by adding the number of graphics (i.e. 10 buttons) with the number of hyperlinks (another 10) making 20 'hits'. Add in the extra graphics that most Web pages have, and you can see that quoting 'hits' is just not valid, even though it has been used to justify the numbers of site visitors quite erroneously – as some investors in dot coms now know only too well.)

The more sites there are that offer much the same as you do (or more than you do) that is of value to the visitors, the fewer real visitor numbers you will get. So, building community (in much the same way that stores issue their own credit cards and points cards) is the only way to counter this – along with perpetually offering more on your site in the way of information or cutting-edge product lines.

It has been roughly calculated that the current ratio of Internet users to websites is five users per site. Even with this rough yardstick you can see that you will have to work very hard to ensure that visitors revisit your site at all.

THE GROWTH OF INTERNET LAW

Lawyers are earning a lot of money with the advent of the Internet. Every transaction on the Internet has, in effect, had legal advice to enable it to happen. Fear, compliance with legal aspects of all the processes that are now being conducted on the Net, and opportunism drive this explosion of work for the legal profession.

The contrast between throwing the rule book out of the window on the one hand and the simple need to protect the rights of customers and attribute the responsibilities of e-commerce companies on the other has started lawyers off in hot discussions on which traditional rules should be set aside and which are essential. In addition, the perpetual updating of agreements in this flexible transitional world creates difficulties in the adaptation of the tried and tested laws. These delays in getting the legal frameworks together have been responsible for the death of some partnership and associateship agreements before they even got off the ground.

Fortunately, some lawyers have learned to reduce the amount of legalese being used and have drafted documents that are short and sweet – and understandable. Some business partnerships have suffered a retrospective disapproval of the legal basis for their partnerships because of this, but conversely, because of the shortcuts taken in providing documentation, they have been able to launch their killer businesses and gain critical mass and community.

It has been very difficult for lawyers because there has not only been a huge learning curve to identify the risks and the basis for use of the Internet within business, but also amazing growth rates both of companies and partnerships being formed. Traditionally, lawyers – both solicitors and barristers – have not been practised in drafting simple agreements quickly, to enable deals to be struck and signed fast. Some lawyers are now providing this service, but an awful lot are rushing to catch up or else say things like 'The Internet will not catch on' or 'I hope that I retire before it gets to us!'

THE EXPERT E-LAWYER

As with all e-commerce and Internet specialists in all other disciplines, the e-lawyer is a busy person. The vast amount of areas on which a law firm would have to advise in relation to the Internet is quite beyond the normal scope of growth in different areas of industry. All the old chestnuts have surfaced – trademarks, copyright, payment, confidentiality, the Data Protection Act – and these and more have to be addressed within the new processes and environments that the Internet and e-commerce bring along as baggage.

Spoofing – or stealing customers from legitimate sites by putting up a bootlegging site that looks and feels like the legitimate site – creates work in myriad areas within traditional business. And there are the obviously untried areas in which precedent has not yet been set. All in all it is a very unsettling period and requires a lot of time to sort out – even if you're not paranoid!

Criminal activity, money laundering, defamation, hacking, the distribution of porn and other muddy and muddled areas all need to be focused upon in order that the wonderful facility the Internet offers is not going to create such barriers that new developments and opportunities cannot be taken. It's really a question of whether lawyers and governments can move fast enough to meet the ever-changing needs and opportunities without driving their clients to distraction.

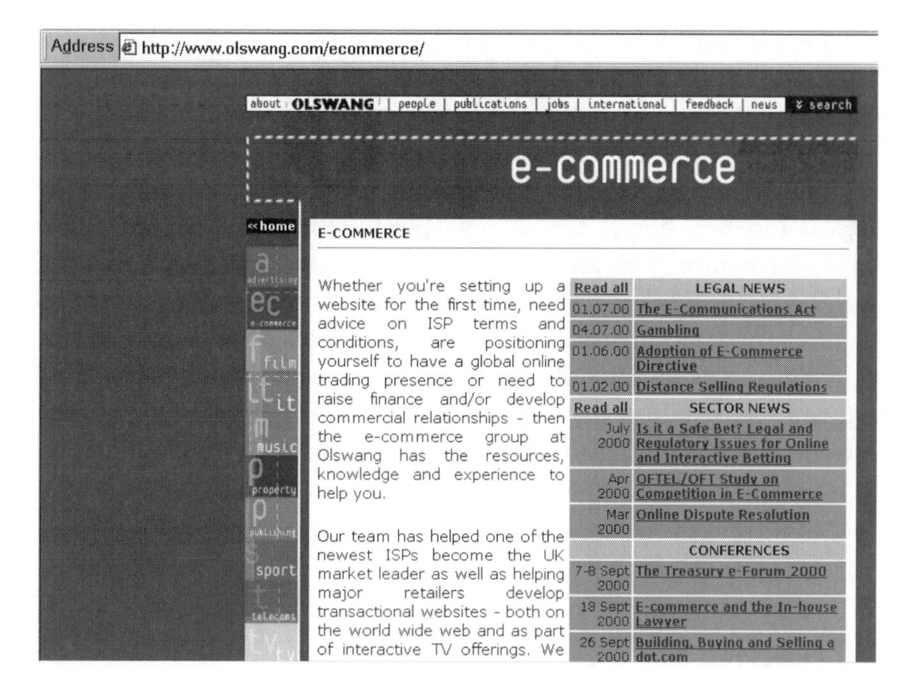

Fig. 9.1 Olswang is one of many law firms who are geared up for the internet

THE LEGAL IMPACT ON E-COMMERCE

The legal questions surrounding e-commerce and the use of Internet technologies form one of the biggest hurdles affecting the growth of commerce on the Internet. What could be a simple partnership agreement could immediately turn into something too expensive for many of the 87 per cent of businesses in the UK who are SMEs (small to medium-sized enterprises) if they have to hire a lawyer to draft a lengthy agreement. As such there are likely to be considerable numbers of partnerships that are based totally on trust, or some minor heads of agreement in the more virtual organisations.

Governments and the law can effectively create major barriers to the development and launch of new Internet-enabled businesses simply by being out of date. Regulation of the Internet in application of standards found in other areas of business could be a two-edged sword both to draft and to regulate. The freedom of the Internet could be constipated by the multiplicity of regulations applicable in different jurisdictions. The lack of cutting-edge knowledge and vision in our politicians and civil servants is likely to be the biggest rock in the bubbling river of the Internet.

One problem is that if I am a small e-business that wants to offer an application that could terminate the existence of a large technology company, should it have any right to stop me? For the Internet to flow smoothly, the answer should be 'no', but the legal meteorite lurking in the ether is that the large company can now legally strangle my ability to partner through the use of exclusionary practices.

There are a variety of these exclusionary practices starting to happen on the Internet, such as charging fees for search engine placement or locked-in distribution of software with new computers. As more of these occur, you will start to see more private actions arise that will provide e-law firms with a significant amount of work.

STICKINESS IN SITES

How do you motivate seasoned Internet users to visit your site repeatedly? It is only when the fundamental decision has been made by your company to provide reliable and convenient service and information that is up to date and pertinent, that you will attract repeated visits because then you will have become a utility. After that it is a matter of creating a habit, because people will always travel the easy, familiar route rather than the unfamiliar.

> **Transition info** eBay keeps its visitors hooked for longer whilst Yahoo! is the most visited Internet site (*The Guardian*, August 2000).

Sitting on the sofa and turning on the TV offers easy information gathering (through the television news channels) and easy entertainment. With websites beginning to be accessed via the TV as well as through mobile phones, in addition to the original plugged-in modem in a PC, different people with different personalities can choose their route to the information. The learned behaviour of the couch potato is satisfied.

Most people still search for information, usually triggered by normal day-to-day events – whether this be for detailed news, or researching costs for prospective purchases, or perhaps a medical need. Beyond that, entertainment and music and then shopping are the biggest attractions. But the biggest seller on the Internet is porn, followed by home shopping, which is on the increase because of the convenience it offers.

INTERNET SHARE-PRICE FLUCTUATIONS AND OVERVALUATION

Since the dot-com bubble was said to have become dot gone, there is nothing that will enable a reclamation of share prices back to those heady days of extraordinary prices on IPO. The public perception of virtual companies has been dented.

Yet just think back to Black Monday, in October 1987, when the market lost more than 20 per cent of its value. It fell in spite of the fact that assets of the vast majority of the largest companies were hard assets or assets that had a realisable market value, such as buildings, equipment, plant and lorries. Imagine what would have happened if those companies didn't have hard assets?

With the advent of the Internet, changing business models and processes, the benchmarks against which share value is judged (such as price earnings ratios), are difficult to justify. The period of adjustment will continue until a new yardstick, and understood business model parameters for different kinds of businesses, are created. No one can accurately value Internet shares.

Interestingly enough, this state of affairs does have its precedents. For instance, when software houses were set up in the 1970s and 1980s the valuations of these companies were extremely difficult to judge because all the assets of the company were the brains of the people. Stock-exchange investors were unhappy with such intangibles, wanting some hard assets to indicate the foundations.

Now, with so many people creating virtual companies with little or no traditional assets, all the boundaries will have to be redrawn yet again.

On the plus side, however, there is little doubt (shown by the numbers of people who are wanting to invest in Internet shares) that IPO values will go up when the business plans stack up. The numbers of companies going for an IPO will also rise again. There are still a few other fledgling Internet companies that have overhyped their potential without a good business model and have withdrawn from IPO 'temporarily' until the market picks up.

Let's try some basic figures:

You sell a CD and make 30p gross.
If, say, you sell 1 million CDs you will make £300,000 gross.
If your overhead is for 20 shops at £1000 per month rent, heat and light, etc. then that will cost you £20,000 per month or £240,000 per year and you'll end up with £60,000, which is taxable.

Now translate that into a cutting-edge on-line business and the necessary distribution centre. You raise £10 million to do that. You're now able to attract around 100 million people and so your dynamics change.

POTENTIAL GROWTH AND PROFIT

We saw in an earlier chapter that Amazon fell from favour when just one analyst downgraded his forecasts of profitability for the company. Was he right?

Well, consider the following argument, which is something along the lines of what Amazon's founder, Jeff Bezos, would undoubtedly be arguing to his backers.

Let's say his company never got any more customers, but that each of its existing customers purchased one book next year with an average mark-up per book of £1. That would give a gross margin on the sales of these books in the region of £12 million. With an investment in its back-end systems of £40 million, the return is therefore around 30 per cent.

Now take into account the growth in new on-line areas such as electronics and auctions, not to mention the fact that new customers are visiting every day. What is clear is that the potential profitability for the future is massive, regardless of whether there are enough hard assets to protect one's investment. Add, also, factors such as critical mass, and being first to market and it is clear why the likes of Amazon are so attractive to investors.

PROVIDING REAL VALUE

With the uncertainty surrounding Internet shares that has appeared, following the corrections within the dot-com marketplace since the turn of the century, it has been much more difficult for organisations to raise capital. Would-be investors are now looking hard and long to determine which offerings are likely to provide real value.

Providing real value is giving the investor a reason to hold or want shares in your company. When you do go to market, providing real value should help to ensure the success of your offering, although this is not always the case. IPO investors can be finicky and sometimes a company with little in the way of value but with a great story will capture the hearts of the investment community ahead of one that provides real value.

Providing value, however, is a long-term growth model. It can be achieved by owning proprietary technology that gives your e-commerce presence something unique, or it can be through an investment in infrastructure such as a distribution chain. Real value can also be provided through the delivery of content on your site – be it intellectual or entertainment – and an application or an on-line service that is difficult or impossible to duplicate. Real value can also be the strength of the on-line community that you create.

HOW TO SURVIVE A SHAKEOUT

A shakeout occurs when a large number of companies are all fighting for a piece of the action in a finite marketplace. Eventually some start to fail because the customers will gravitate towards a few companies with a better image or product offering. These firms can then buy up smaller firms in the same market and eventually only one or two remaining companies will exist.

It's a sad fact, therefore, that unless you grow fast enough or take on more risk, you will eventually be taken out of the market by those organisations that grow substantially, thanks to the dynamics of the shakeout. Your best protection in a shakeout is to not over-extend your organisation by taking on the added risk of large expansion, unless and until you are ready for it.

Having said that, many a start-up organisation can see the advantages of being bought up by others. It may well be prudent to plan your strategy with the aim of selling out a successful small organisation within, say, two or three years, rather than being unrealistic in believing you can fight your way all the way to the top.

So all in all there are plenty of rocks and boulders in the cyberstream of e-commerce; equally, there are plenty of opportunities. Where you position your e-commerce organisation is critical to its future survival. Knowing which options to select or which paths to follow is the $64,000 question.

Keeping in tune with the world of e-commerce, whether by hiring technically competent staff or learning it yourself, is critical to the future direction of your business and its long-term survival.

10

COPING WITH LEGACIES

Legacies are not always beneficial. We've noted more than once that it's the pioneers who set the rules when trading in a new market environment, leaving others to following in their wake. It's true, of course, that some pioneers suffer from being first, since they have to make the inevitable mistakes as part of their learning process, whereas others can sit in the wings, vulture-like, and learn the lessons without having to go through the painful process of cutting virgin ground and making the mistakes the first time around.

Equally true, there are many others in the new Net economy who are pulled into e-commerce well before they are ready; whilst there are yet other companies held up by their current existing systems or legacy system technologies – known as legacies.

To put it a little clearer, the main problem when tying into legacy systems is effectively connecting the website to a back-end database used by the company, perhaps, as a main driver within the traditional business. Obviously it is important not to put at risk your data when connecting your database to the Web. Equally important is not to confuse your customers by giving them defective information because the link to the data is not reliable.

Eurostar is one company that could have avoided a lot of bad comment when it first created a Web presence. In January 1999, for instance, were you to have looked up the Eurostar website to find the timetable for trains going from Waterloo to Paris you would have seen (if you had looked very carefully) a notice to the effect that the timetable being shown actually ran out in September 1998. That was not particularly helpful; nor was the fact that even if you had known the times of the Paris trains, there would have been no way of booking a ticket on-line, other than by ringing the telephone number shown – which still wouldn't have helped you on a Sunday since the booking office was closed.

We're glad to report that things have changed dramatically since then, with the present Eurostar website giving up-to-date information and allowing bookings to be made straightforwardly. It is clear that the site now ties in to the back-office systems, allowing the customer to experience first-rate service without the need for any personal intervention whatsoever.

Another early starter – this time in the banking business – also had its fair share of problems. If you had been a night worker who happened to bank with Lloyds you might have welcomed the provision of its banking services over the Web. In fact, it would appear to have been an ideal arrangement since the chances of using the bank's daytime services might well have been extremely limited for you.

What a pity, therefore, that if you had logged on to the Lloyds website you would have seen a notice informing you that the service was not available between midnight and 4.00 am. (Later it changed the announcement to tell you that service was available from 4.00 am

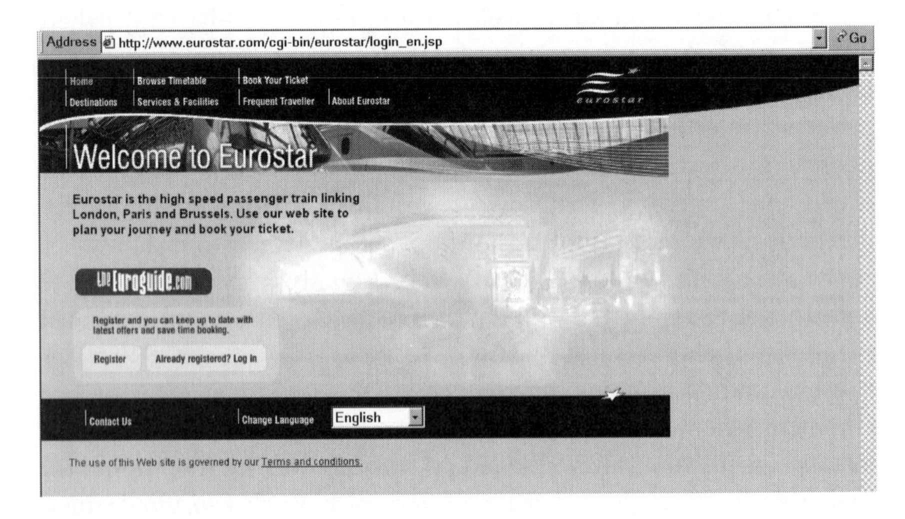

Fig. 10.1 French curves grace Eurostar's tactile site

till midnight – a clear case, perhaps, of someone in the bank's PR department emphasising the good news?)

> **Transition stats** At least 40 per cent of Internet users don't have a clue how to find the websites they want (Lloyds TSB).

The problem undoubtedly arose because of legacy systems getting in the way. Reconciliation of accounts is carried out at night by the banking community and it was not unreasonable to expect there to be a time of day when access to accounts – under the old model – would not be possible (presumably whilst the banks were running end-of-day routines and updates). But the Internet forced Lloyds to update its legacy system, and today (under its new moniker of Lloyds TSB) you can bank on-line at any time of the day or night.

Fig. 10.2 Lloyds TSB – a soft approach to banking

The change of heart and the rush to get a 24-hour operation at Lloyds may not have had anything to do with the management's commitment to giving customer service. In a swingeing attack on business intransigence during April 2000, for instance, the *Financial Times* reported:

> The determination of banks and other financial service companies to 'own the customer relationship', even if that

> means inconveniencing the customer, is opening the way to a new generation of services offering personalised web sites that combine details of their on-line accounts, credit cards, and travel services, all in one place.

As Dennis Keeling, CEO of the suppliers group Business and Accountancy Software Developers Association put it, UK banks were e-commerce dinosaurs, fearing that the onset of rapid electronic reconciliation would make it too easy for customers to switch banks. 'With new players getting into retail Net banking, it will change this cosy little world [of UK banks],' he said.

One of the new players that Keeling must have had at the back of his mind was First-e which was launched in the UK in September 1999. It does its business entirely on-line, and is based in Ireland, even though it operates on behalf of a private French bank, Banque d'Escompte.

First-e offers the full range of standard and specialised banking services such as deposit accounts, cheque books, transfers, credit cards and share trading. In addition, by contracting out to third party companies, it offers property services, life assurance, general insurance and unit trusts. On this basis, First-e assured its customers that they would have access to the best products from leading professionals in each category.

The likes of First-e, Intelligent Finance (the Internet banking arm of Halifax), Cahoot (Abbey National) and Prudential's Egg – none of which are shackled by expensive branch networks – have started to give the high street banks a bloody nose. Fears amongst investors that the banks are no longer as competitive as their new upstart rivals have caused many to jump ship, bailing out of banking stocks and looking around for better deals.

The Sunday Times in July 2000 reported one analyst as saying:

> Customer apathy at being ripped off is starting to disappear through the advent of telephone and Internet banking and the high street banks will find it increasingly tough, and not before time … The problems now reflect in part the deep-rooted arrogance of the traditional banks, which believed that customer loyalty did not require investment in technology.

It has become clear that some of the best banking deals now available are restricted to the Net. We shouldn't be surprised, since it costs about 10 times more for a bank to service a customer who uses branches, than one who uses the Internet.

Meanwhile the 'Big Four' are left pondering their future as they have finally come to realise that a bank created entirely for the Internet, without the costs of an expensive branch network, is able to offer higher rates of interest than its traditional high-street competitors. Of these 'Big Four', HSBC is an interesting example because its foray into Internet banking was launched through access via digital TV and Open. This new access route actually opened the door for HSBC to attract a new set of customers – and one the other banks were not currently targeting: the home-bound non-computer user. Open and Sky digital appealed to a completely new sector of the market who were not used to the faster access speeds of modems via PC and unfriendly keyboards. Niche marketing was the key to this success.

Whilst the banks are finally learning their lessons, other sectors have been licking their wounds and belatedly learning from their mistakes.

Picture the scene. The 'flu has hit you hard and it's all you can do to fall out of bed in the morning. Your pet moggie, unaware that life's priorities have suddenly changed, is miaowing for his fix of Whiskas. You stagger downstairs to the kitchen only to find that you are fresh out of cat food (you didn't have time with the overrunning meeting last night to pop into the store on the way home).

Well, you've heard about Sainsbury's website so you stagger over to your computer and whirr it up into action. After all, if Sainsbury's can deliver a few tins of cat food at least you can keep moggie quiet for a little.

Imagine, then, your disappointment on logging on to Sainsbury's site to find that before you can order anything on-line you first will have to make a physical trip to your local supermarket and meet one of the managers who will accompany you around the store asking you to pinpoint the kinds of things you might like to order in the future. They then will check your credit details and only then will you be allowed to order on-line!

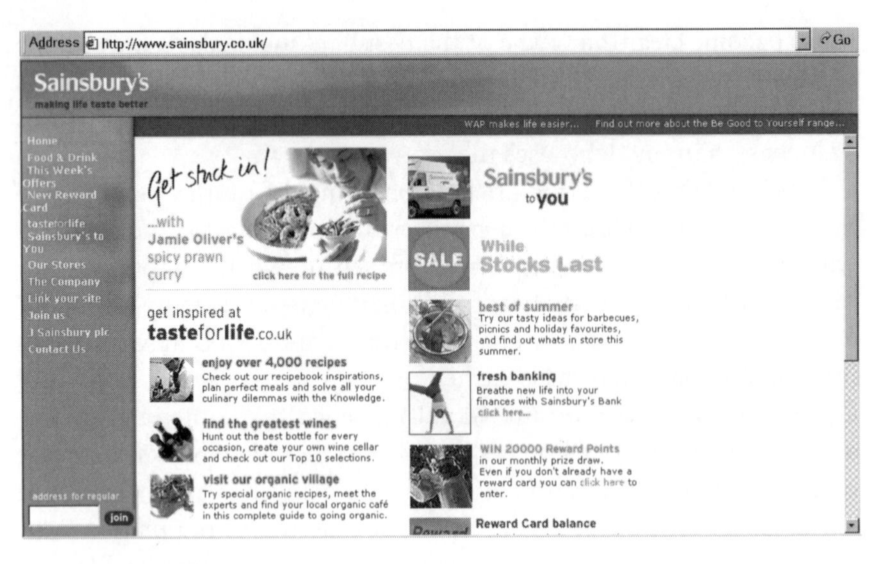

Fig. 10.3 Sainsbury's revamped

However, in 1999 Sainsbury's reviewed this practice and developed a new site that works a great deal better and doesn't insist that you visit them first.

(Cat lovers who were upset by our little story should not worry. Not only was it fictional, but our hero could just as easily have dialled up Tesco Direct which has no such barriers – although along with the 'success' of having over £125 million sales every year, Tesco Direct now finds it is often unable to deliver on the same day whilst it adjusts and gauges supply and demand.)

It was clear that Sainsbury's had wanted to get its customers in front of its products first, and it also set up its operations so as to be able to distribute from large centralised distribution centres. That meant that many areas of the country could not be served – whereas Tesco used its individual stores as the front for Tesco Direct, which meant that wherever it had a large store it could service an area with a radius of some 15 miles from that location.

Transition stats Tesco launched its e-commerce site early in 1999 as an 11-store pilot and developed the business quickly. In the summer of 2000 it had over 100 outlets attracting some 250,000 customers, and by the end of the year planned to have a service operating from 300 stores.

Tesco claims to be the number-one on-line supermarket and this hasn't gone unnoticed by its smaller rivals. Iceland, for instance, re-branded all its 760 stores so that the sign above its doors reads Iceland.co.uk – reinforcing the fact to its clientele that it also has a website. Both Somerfield and Budgen, on the other hand, gave up the unequal struggle and after a few months closed down their on-line offerings.

A food retail analyst with SG Securities, Mike Dennis, warns that supermarkets will only keep their pioneer advantages if they realise that they need to deliver more than food. The lesson from the USA is that those that are thriving are only doing so by getting involved in other activities such as laundry and dry-cleaning services, video rental and water delivery.

Meanwhile Jim Norton at the Institute of Directors warns that too many retail businesses are built around the value of in-store transactions. He foresees a time when there will be a split between the buying of perishable and non-perishable goods, with the latter being bought locally whilst non-perishables are bought as regular repeat orders over the Internet. 'There will be no brand loyalty with these bulk purchases and less need to visit vast out-of-town supermarket sites,' he warned.

Although boasting a high turnover, Tesco is the only UK supermarket already running its e-commerce site in the black. This is mainly due to the fact that it has bolted on its distribution to its store operations, so costs are effectively cut back. In stark contrast, Sainsbury's and Asda/Walmart are both further developing their depot-based systems. The lesson is clear. If Tesco makes a success of Tesco Direct, we could see its out-of-town stores become glorified distribution centres and this could become the pattern for the other supermarket pioneers.

What these on-line supermarket wars and bank rivalry clearly demonstrate is the fact that traditional bricks-and-mortar businesses need to migrate to a clicks-and-mortar operation if they are to succeed at all. Legacy systems that lock their companies into the past ages do no favours at all, and could cost these retail dinosaurs their very survival.

Meanwhile, another sector of the retail economy is feeling the chill wind from over the pond, as we'll see in the next chapter.

11

MORE CHANGED BUSINESS MODELS

Car sales in the USA will never be the same again; The Internet has seen to that.

It wasn't long ago that the new and used car salesperson was a familiar figure on American TV's advertising spots and in the movies. Every car lot had a quirky figure – often wearing some outlandish gear – extolling to the couch potatoes the virtues of buying a car from their emporium. Not only could you buy your dream machine from this paragon of American consumerism, but they would also offer you a trade-in for your old car, arrange a finance deal for you and even fix your insurance.

That may soon be a thing of the past. The secret to the sales reps' business was that they were able to offer superb deals on their new cars by buying them in bulk at a discount, subsidising the sale price from the commissions they were making on the finance deals and insurance. The second-hand cars added little to their bottom line profits, but they sold the finance and insurance on those too!

So pity the poor reps who woke up one morning to discover that their customers were now buying their new cars on-line at a discount; selling their second-hand cars in on-line auctions; getting cheap insurance deals through the Internet and – yes – getting their loans on-line as well. The reps' USP, and their margins, had disappeared virtually overnight.

What our American friends started to experience over two years ago is already happening here in the UK. Many predicted that the UK car sales model wouldn't be affected for about four years after the USA had changed, but after only 18 months the papers were full of stories about car imports from Europe being sold on the Internet at massive discounts, car auctions seeing the price of second-hand cars falling dramatically, and of the harsh new economic climate for car dealers.

Dixons Motors teamed up with Direct Line Insurance to supply new cars, second-hand cars, insurance and finance from the one site; Virgin Cars launched its site offering to sell models at a 30 per cent discount on showroom prices; DC Cook Holdings upped the ante by offering discounts of 40 per cent.

And getting in on the act, the Consumers Association discovered that by using the Internet 'with minimal effort cars can be bought for thousands of pounds less'.

The car manufacturers started to experience the chill winds of a new consumer backlash. In a vain attempt at stemming the tide, Vauxhall offered £1000 off its showroom prices on its Internet site for people who bought on-line, but were surely disappointed to find that only 250 customers took up their offer in four months – an indication, perhaps, that the car giant was out of tune with its customers and market forces?

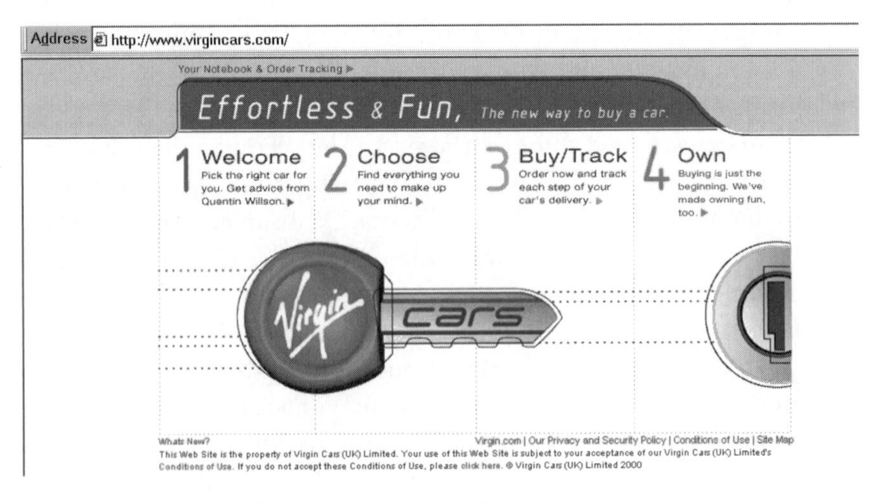

Fig. 11.1 Virgin offers a key to on-line car sales

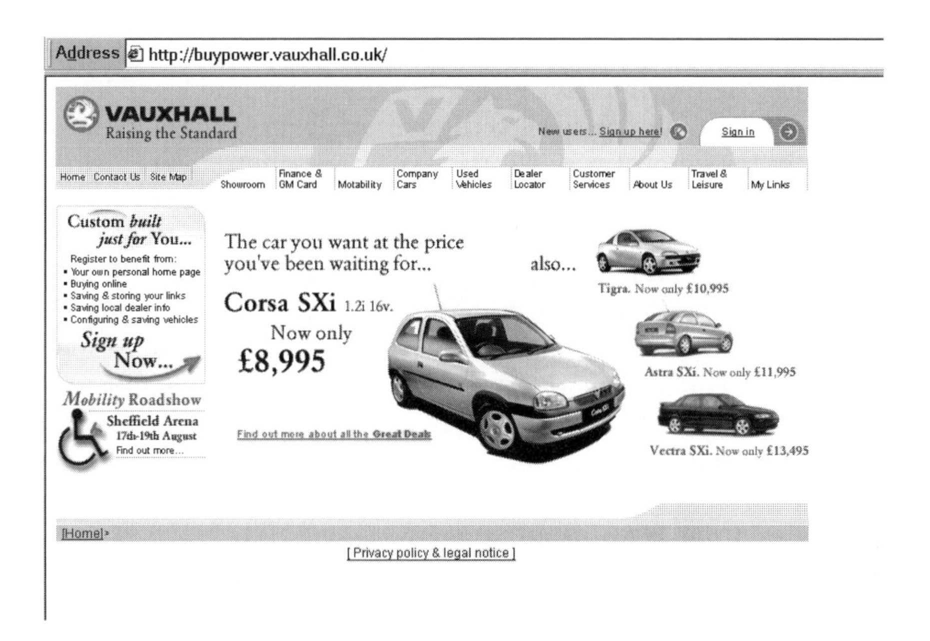

Fig. 11.2 Vauxhall's on-line brochure

By the summer of 2000 some of the car dealerships had started to fight back with large discounts that in many cases undercut the new Internet business start-ups. Reg Vardy, for instance, offered a Nissan Primera for £8995 compared with Jamjar.com's £9137.

In addition, a number of papers reported that there was evidence that UK dealers were deliberately paying less for continentally sourced used cars, when they were part-exchanged, in order to protect their own businesses. In some cases these continentally sourced cars had a trade-in value of up to 30 per cent less than equivalent cars bought from UK dealers.

At the time of writing it is too early to say what the overall long-term effect of the Internet will be on the UK's car sales model. If the American experience is anything to go by, however, it is clear that by the time the Office of Fair Trading sorts out the alleged car-dealer cartels sporting artificially high prices, it will be too late anyway; and this rear-guard action by the dealers may well be seen as the final twitching of an aged dinosaur being introduced to reality by the new businesses processes the Internet is forcing on every aspect of commercial life.

What is now the computer giant Dell was one of the first to take advantage of the Internet as a communications and distribution channel. When Michael Dell started off his empire the traditional computer sales model was that the hardware manufacturers distributed their PCs through an established network of distributors, who sold them on to resellers, who sold them on to end users.

Dell realised that if he was to sell his computers directly to the end users, he could cut out the distributors and resellers and end up with a much higher profit margin. The end users would also gain because they could be offered some of these savings, and they would get their computers delivered faster. The only ones to lose out would be the distributors and resellers.

Who'd have thought it? In the early days, Michael Dell simply bought Compaq PCs in bulk and rebadged them with his own logo. In effect he was a broker of PCs.

With the arrival of the Internet Dell was able to extend his sales and distribution model such that today it is the busiest and most successful business website in the world. Every day the site generates some $18 million-worth of sales and it has a market capitalisation of around $16 billion.

Dell discovered something else that even he wasn't expecting from his site. In order to offer an incentive for people to buy on-line he offered a discount of 1 per cent on his website over and above the prices he was quoting on his traditional mail-order business. It turned out that when the potential customers arrived at his site, the 'kiddies-in-the-sweet-shop' syndrome kicked in whereby the customers actually 'upsold' themselves.

No longer was it necessary to have a salesperson effectively talking up a sale to encourage the end user to opt for a more expensive machine. The customers did it themselves, simply by being shown all the options they could choose for their PC. As each option was ticked or unticked, the end price changed automatically so that the customers could immediately see what combination of extras they could afford, and mix and match them until they were happy.

So the customers upsold themselves, they were happy because they convinced themselves they had a bargain, and to crown it all Dell put

Fig. 11.3 Dell is the king of all e-commerce sites

a priority on customer service so that any queries were answered promptly and he ended up with happy customers who all went away and told their friends.

What Dell, as a successful Net entrepreneur, demonstrated only too well was that a business should be strategy- and business-driven – relying on available technology, but not driven by the technology.

Food retailing is no different in this respect from computers or car sales. *Computer Weekly* magazine in June 2000 reported that the poultry products supplier Bernard Matthews was about to go on-line with expected savings of tens of thousands of pounds a year by investing in an on-line order information service.

This was no on-line service for housewives, however; the service was instead set up to provide the company with up-to-the-minute stock and sales details in three of the UK's largest supermarket chains. Whenever a supermarket changes its order for BM's poultry, managers can be alerted by mobile phone so that they can make the necessary changes in the production line process as quickly as possible. With factory labour costs running at £35 million a year, even small savings in efficiency can make massive savings on the bottom line of the profit and loss account.

The Internet allows the traditional process (which involves reconciling data from three different systems) to be collapsed from a three-hour operation into something that takes just minutes.

If final proof were needed about the impact that the Internet is having on business processes, then look no further than the stock markets to see which companies are 'sexy' and which are out of favour. In July 2000 *The Sunday Times* asked investment experts in the Square Mile to name the shares they regarded as 'must-have' shares from around the world.

Of the 10 listed, seven reflected the potential offered by Internet enablement, including the future potential of WAP (wireless application protocol, driving the convergence of mobile telephony with the Internet). Top of the UK's must-have shares was Vodaphone (which is leading development of data transfer from computers to phones); on Nasdaq, it was Sun Microsystems (which effectively drives the

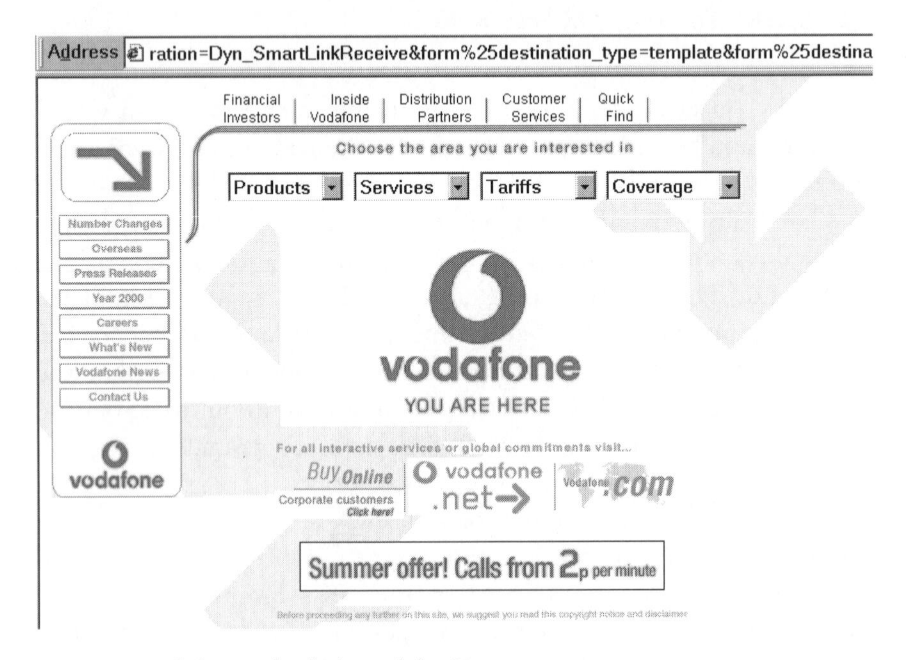

Fig. 11.4 *Vodafone is the darling of the City*

Internet and the telecoms revolution) and Cisco (providing the hardware for the Internet to work); in Hong Kong the leader was China Mobile (attracting one million new users a month); and in Paris it was Vivendi (which is involved with providing Internet access through digital TV).

The message once again is clear. Every business needs to think very seriously how the Internet is likely to affect it. In particular, who will be threatening *your* business in the months ahead?

12

PREDICTIONS CAN BE WRONG

We've seen that in this Internet age the biggest threat to traditional bricks and mortar stores is the out-of-town, out-of-county, out-of-country predator who no-one sees coming until it is too late. Does this mean that every business needs forever to be looking over its shoulder – a cyber-Caesar looking for Brutus's cyber-sword?

Well, yes it does. Who, after all, 10 years ago, could have predicted the changes in car retailing, or book selling, or food retailing ... or the way in which people relate in on-line communities?

Who, for that matter, could have predicted that the virtual auctioneer ebay.com could even have considered bidding £1 billion for Sotheby's?

And who would have believed them if they had? We all know that so-called 'experts' regularly get their predictions wrong? And some are never allowed to forget them! Amongst our all-time favourite predictions:

- 'There is a world market for maybe five computers' (Chairman, IBM, 1948);
- 'In the future, computers may weigh no more that $1\frac{1}{2}$ tonnes' (*Popular Mechanics*, 1949);

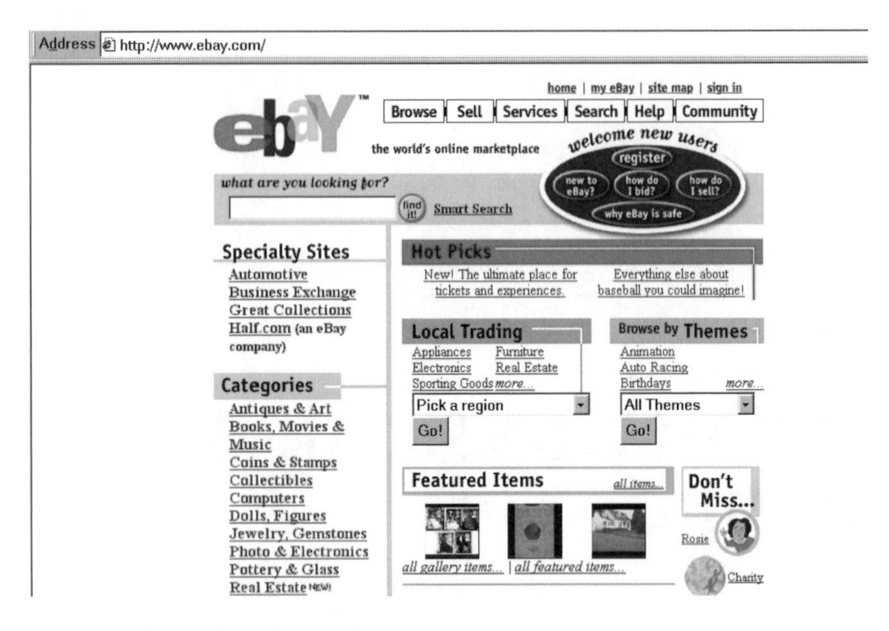

Fig. 12.1 ebay is the world leader in on-line auctions

- 'There is no reason why anyone would want a computer in their home' (Chairman, Digital Equipment Corporation, 1977).

Hang on a minute. That last one is well within the lifetime of most of us!

> **Ostriches?** Dot com start-ups and old economy companies embracing the Internet are dangerously complacent about the threat posed by each other. About 41 per cent say they do not see any competitive threat emerging, even after 10 years (*The Times*, August 2000).

We'll see in a moment that as distribution channels change, so too must you change your business model and processes.

13

CHANGES IN COMMUNICATIONS AND DISTRIBUTION CHANNELS

The Internet changes everything. Yes, it does. Even the things you don't think it ought to affect will change. The introduction of new distribution channels has led to startling developments and overlapping platforms. Now your television screen looks like your PC monitor and vice versa, and phones are able to show cut-down versions of Internet sites or even receive verbal versions of the same content. This allows customers to access the information they want when they want it and where they want it and it opens up tremendous business opportunities for access and distribution in a multi-platform environment.

Bloomberg Television has developed in exactly this way and offers multiple patches of information on a single television screen. The familiar newsreader sitting at a desk, reading to camera, has the dominant portion of the screen. A tickertape runs along the bottom of the screen and there are other areas of perpetually changing headlines, together with scrolling rolling data run by all the time.

So, you have several pieces of information being broadcast at once. Bloomberg also focuses specifically on City, finance and business activities and so it addresses a niche market. The formula is successful. The information attracts a wide audience who can assimilate the larger picture in the financial arena in a short time-frame because of the multiple simultaneous broadcasting.

Many television sets now allow you to bring up 'windows' and watch several channels at once, selecting a dominant one on which you will also receive sound. This means that you can configure your television set to emulate the style of Bloomberg broadcasting, but select channels and programmes that are entirely of your choosing.

Bloomberg was bound to launch an Internet version of its service which could be personalised by the user in order to complete the loop. It offers the same facilities as well as enhancement, available thanks to the browser technology available on PCs, and gives customers exactly what news and information they want, when they want it. The next step for Bloomberg was to capture the mobile phone market too. Then the Bloomberg customer (and potential Bloomberg customer) could get what information they wanted, when they wanted it and where they wanted it. And Bloomberg got the market positioning it wanted too.

So the business models change, and the costs of the different areas change too. The distribution of information on the Bloomberg formula is very different from that of the printed page. But the newspaper and book publishing businesses, which have fed lumps of information and entertainment to us up until now, are changing too.

Take a quick look at some book publishers, such as Pearson, and how they are repositioning themselves after acquisitions in 1999, to exploit the Internet to give them pole position – again in an easily identifiable niche market.

When Pearson announced it was to buy National Computer Systems (which provides on-line testing services for American schools) for £1.7 billion the plan was to integrate NCS with Pearson Education's Learning Network and to distribute it via America Online. The financing for this deal was through the largest rights issue seen to date in Britain at the time of writing. The rights issue was aimed at minimising both underwriting costs and the risk of sudden market swings and offered shareholders three new shares for every eleven owned at a large discount.

'Webucation', such as the Pearson Education Learning Network, gives an opportunity to step back and review the old and more modern attitudes to education and note the advantages of on-line learning. E-learning is a sector with almost unlimited potential for growth. Indeed, having made this acquisition, Pearson has placed itself right at the centre of this relatively new industry, focusing its core business on education rather than general and educational hard-copy publishing.

This development is likely to bring concerns that the education e-revolution could mean that teachers are perceived as 'abdicating responsibility' by placing too much reliance on the new technology over old-fashioned teaching methods. Some would argue that children are at greater risk because of a reduction of access to the 'precious' relationship between teacher and pupil. In addition, there are possibilities of potentially creating a wider educational divide between those who have knowledge and those who don't, because of the sheer lack of motivation of some people to learn remotely or on-line. It is a teaching and people-management tradition that learning is more consistent when there is a one-to-one or up to one-to-30 teacher : pupil ratio.

There will be some discomfiture in any change. Therefore it will be essential to build the right balance between these two methods of distributing education and ensure that the perceptions of the public, as well as those being educated, are properly addressed. It will also be important to judge the quality and quantity of results in an on-going manner.

Saving bottom-line cost – by not going through the traditional publishing routine for hard copy, as well as opening up larger distribution channels – is obviously the objective Pearson has. However, this will not be without its additional costs, which must include awareness raising and calming the fears of those who worry about losing the teacher/pupil relationship.

In the retail arena there are magnificent opportunities too, but there are equally, enormous threats – of death.

The Christmas of 1999 was a bumper year for sales on-line. The most heavily sold item was the CD. CDs have advantages over many other items as presents – their uniform size and light weight makes them eminently postable.

This bonanza was wonderful for the on-line CD retailers like Amazon and CDNow but it rang warning bells for those terrestrial megastores of portable media that have been making large sales for

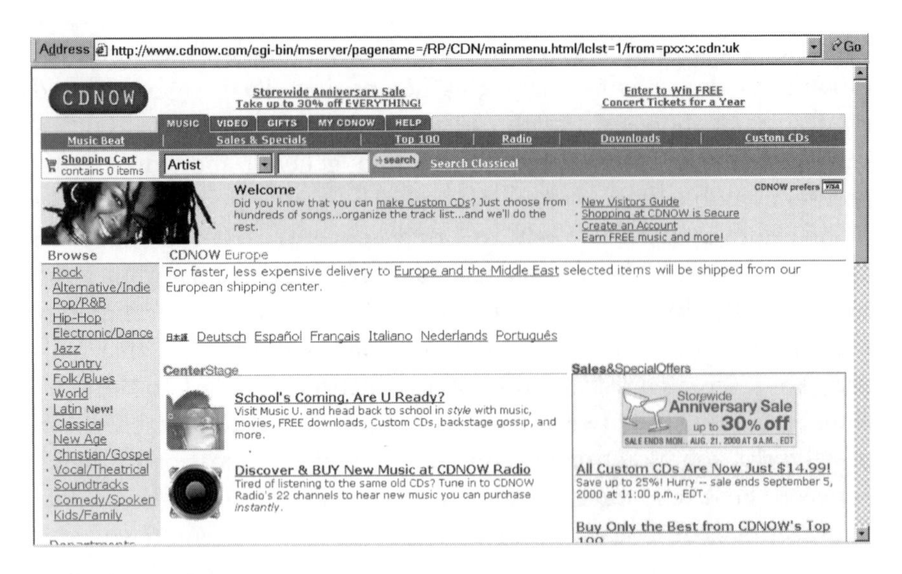

Fig. 13.1 CDNow became a global brand whilst others were only waking up to the fact of e-commerce

some years of CDs, tapes, videos and the like. As Virgin/HMV stated in March 2000, a 10 per cent swing away from the high street stores in CD sales alone would mean that the bricks-and-mortar megastores would no longer be viable. The on-line trade was wiping out their profit margin.

Businesses and business models have to be transformed. They have to embrace Internet technologies throughout their businesses – or die. It really is as simple and as frightening as that.

If you are to looking for an e-commerce or e-business strategy to tack on to your existing business, then please think again. What you need to do is start from the premise that you must see every opportunity within your business to use Internet technologies. All your people must have an 'e' (a bit like the BT advert of yesteryear in which Maureen Lipman was happy if her grandson had an 'ology').

This is a tough decision to follow through. Yet some of our major corporations have bitten the bullet and abandoned their top-down hierarchical structures in order to let new recruits and young blades teach and mentor established managers and directors – a complete turn-about of the traditional roles and role models. Because the Internet changes everything it is essential to change the way we work as well as the processes. And that starts with understanding and ownership.

One of the bastions of what many would think was the old guard has done just that. General Electric (GE) is a traditional business that has integrated e-commerce principles and practice into every part of the business. In fact its Chief Executive, Jack Welch, commented: 'Any company, old or new, that does not see this technology as important as breathing could be on its last breath.' To GE the Internet is an essential new medium for business success. We could all emulate the GE philosophy and model and come up trumps in so doing.

The tendency with a new technology is to set up a division to deal with it; so in the past there were IT divisions to deal with information technology, and MIS departments to provide the management information services, and – more latterly – knowledge departments to manage knowledge within companies too. In truth, the value of any of these essential elements in a business is neither perceived nor realised until they are integrated so far into the way the business lives and breathes that everyone in the company 'owns' and has responsibility for them.

Knowledge management can never work unless all the people share both the input and the output. It will always be skewed if a

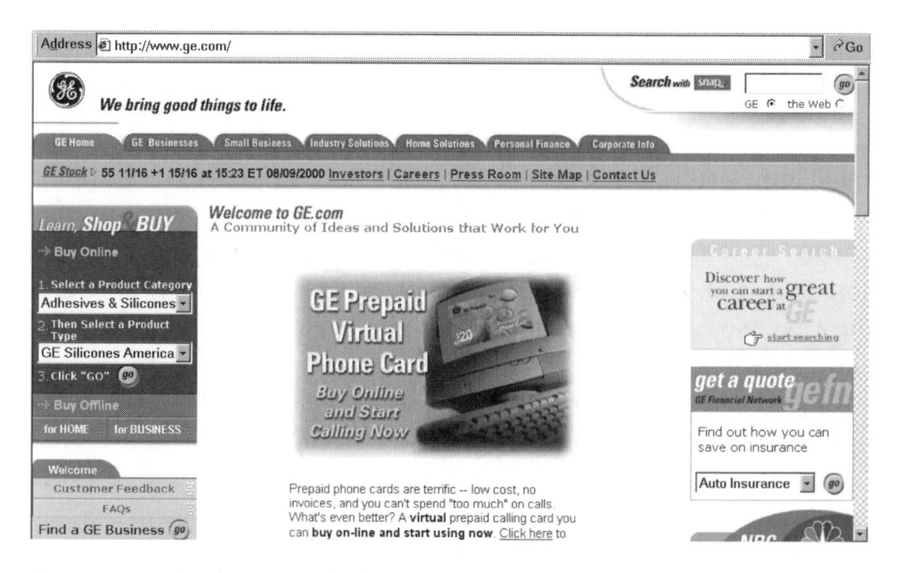

Fig. 13.2 GE has been completely reinvented exploiting Internet technologies

single department has control and acts as a funnel for the rest of the business. The same applies to e-commerce and Internet technologies – unless everyone is involved then it won't work and the business will be roaring away in some areas whilst others are stuck in treacle. The imbalances will cripple the business and the costs will rise because of the dysfunction.

What GE did was:

- decided that all the top managers (600) should understand e-business;
- developed a mentoring programme for them using younger people as their 'buddies' to teach them about the Internet;
- in return mentored the 'buddies' on the principles of what business in GE was all about;
- set up continental and regional e-commerce committees to facilitate best practice;
- actively embraced ideas and broke the culture where raising ideas was frowned upon and could set you up for a put-down;
- put all of this into a corporate mandate, with customer feedback and input as well as go-getting leadership for action.

GE have found that the whole company now comes up with ideas. Greater understanding of other people's work has been achieved and it is difficult to tell, within discussions, which are the marketing people or managers or computing and IT people.

In the fast-moving world driven by the opportunities offered by the Internet, ideas have to be acted upon as soon as they are born. Long evaluation processes are just not viable because there isn't time for them if the ideas are to be acted upon before other people go for them. As Jack Welch put it, 'We have to pounce, every day.' As the company and its top managers are of one mind on this, ideas and their assessment and implementation become part of the way of life and, therefore, moderately easy.

GE identified a checklist of 10 steps which it told to David Bicknell of *Computer Weekly* in June 2000:

1 Have a powerful, committed business champion.
2 Involve customers throughout the effort.
3 Get top-down support.

4. Create a neutral electronic environment.
5. Don't wait until everything is perfect. Just begin.
6. Establish 'stretch' goals and be ambitious.
7. Get business user buy-in and participation.
8. Find suppliers whose commitment matches your own.
9. Cut the red tape. Stop at nothing.
10. Follow up with customers after the launch.

Perhaps, having seen how straightforward the basic principles are and that they don't throw up obvious difficulties in implementation, we should make this philosophy and practice the basis for assessing and using any new ideas and technologies. However, remember that by automating the processes quite a number of them will not follow one on the other at completion like end-of-day routines. In fact things like backing up and recovering data will have to be done without taking the system off-line – as will any maintenance.

Philip Evans and Thomas Wurster, co-leaders of the Boston Consulting Group's media and convergence practice, hone down the basic advantages of the Internet to those of reach, richness and affiliation (*Harvard Business Review*, December 1999):

- *Reach* applies simply to the numbers of customers and potential customers who can be accessed (and therefore within reach) as well as the number of products and services that can be offered to them. Instead of being limited by geographical location and storage space, as one would be in high-street retailing, many thousands of products can be offered to many millions of customers.

- *Richness* applies to the depth of information that is being offered and can provide customers with a greater knowledge, whilst also acquiring information about the customer. A book or music site can provide independent reviews as well as photos of artistes and authors along with biographies and anecdotal information – all of which could help the customer to decide to buy. Capturing information about the customers whilst they are searching, as well as identifying the types of products purchased, builds up a profile for future marketing.

- A focus on *affiliation* is essential because with the Internet affiliations change. Whereas pushing brand has been thought to be vital

> to gaining customer purchase in terrestrial stores that have a shortage of display space, on the Internet all visitors (business or consumer) can navigate and search to find a product by its function or fulfilment of a specific need, so the customer is likely to reign supreme and affiliations change. The interests of the customer have to be of paramount importance by getting the best deal or finding the right solution. For instance, if you look at Lastminute.com, it offers you the ability to bid for a flight by selecting your departure and arrival airports and dates of travel and then putting in a bid for the air tickets. Lastminute will put your bid in for you and, until such time as you are told you are successful, you won't know which airline's ticket you will be buying. Air travel, in these circumstances, becomes a utility.

As with everything e-commerce, you can chew the fat over these three maxims, but you must revisit them as things develop, and revise your ideas. But to succeed, the in-depth focus on your core business issues is the next bit of fun!

PART 3

GETTING YOUR HOUSE IN ORDER

14

CORE BUSINESS ISSUES

With so many opportunities to tune up all the business processes it is difficult to know where to start. There are mindset adjustments needed just in assessing what needs to be done, by when and by whom.

Firstly, when assessing the business case of your intended e-commerce venture, the ability to see the general picture as well as the detail is essential. If you are intending to start up a company then the normal business planning has to be gone through very carefully. If you need a template to run up a business plan then log on to **www.e-biz-pro.org/bizplan.htm** and download one that will give you a memory-jogging crib sheet for the words – for an executive plan and expanded plan as well as the profit and loss account (P&L), budget and cash-flow spreadsheets – and their attendant notes.

Transition stats At least 64 per cent of businesses still don't use e-commerce as a sales channel.

If you're intending to introduce Internet technologies to your bricks-and-mortar company the first thing you are likely to do is decide that you need to have a website. This, even if it is a simple 'shop window' site for your business, will help you get your corporate head in order as to what using the Web does to traditional business patterns.

You'll find that on-line shoppers – both consumers and businesses – are expecting more of the sites they visit now than they did a year ago. Therefore if your site is too clever or too slow then they'll be unlikely to revisit it. Actually, a bad website can be disastrous to a business. Professional and effective Web design is absolutely crucial for e-commerce. However, many companies think that they can get a site up on the Web without bearing in mind those factors that may put their customers off.

The user interface must be good. If not then the site will lose business for the company and every lost customer could be worth quite a lot. If you think of it in strictly commercial terms the loss is of a customer who has come to find your business. For example, say the customer was one who phoned the company up, asked for information and was subsequently left hanging on the switchboard or put through to the wrong people. The impression of the company is that it is incompetent and doesn't care enough to keep its customers satisfied. Having a good user interface therefore is a must.

Beyond that, navigation is a key element of this. Visitors have to be able to find whatever they want within three clicks of the mouse, from anywhere else on your site. This may sound like a tall order, but not providing information for customers as easily as this will drive customers away.

Lots of sites have brilliantly conceived graphics and fail miserably in their interaction with users because they are effectively showing off technical prowess rather than giving users ease of use. One of the most regularly encountered problems is the slow download, which generates both frustration and boredom. This is usually because too many graphics are on the site and they are not optimised so as to download quickly. Lack of thought as to how the visitor to the site is going to view what they see also means that there is often nothing for the user to read whilst graphics are downloading. Text can be there very fast and can aid information transfer before the graphics come in to play.

Shoppers are regularly frustrated because of the design of some leading e-commerce sites. Many on-line shoppers even abandon making a purchase because of this. Many silly errors can contribute to this, and there is no excuse for websites that are deficient, because there is a vast array of software tools available to enable the most complicated as well as the most simple of tasks. However, the deficiencies exist mainly, we think, because of bad planning and lack of customer/user focus.

For instance, it is business suicide not to provide:

- a check-out button to enable purchasers who have made a selection to effect the transaction;
- an automatic e-mail button for contacting the company;
- a means whereby the visitors can ask for more information on products and services;
- a search tool of some kind;
- fast downloads without having to go for plug-ins;
- sites that are downloadable on a 28-kbps modem.

But we don't want to frighten you too much. After all, it's planning and thinking the processes through that will save any company from such rudimentary errors. However, if you want to get a snapshot of how a site fares, log on to **www.e-biz-pro.org** once again, this time for a free benchmark test – then you can get a quick assessment of what you need to address.

For e-commerce you'll need to buy flat-pack-shop and other turnkey software. There is some excellent stuff around that stands the test of time and costs very little considering its functionality. The alternative is simply to go to a good developer and check them out as to what they have designed before, speaking to their customers and looking at the sites they have turned out.

There is a growing market for hosted e-commerce services that get over the problem of your needing up-to-the-minute in-house IT and Internet knowledge. After all, small and medium-sized businesses have all the same problems experienced by the large companies – but they don't have the same resources. There are also really savvy agencies around now who will consult for you, hand-holding you through this minefield of new things.

Selecting these is all a matter of finding a balance between reinventing the wheel, getting the whole thing up and running quickly, and an easy start-up to which you can add functionality easily as the site develops. Key issues here are:

- flexibility
- not reinventing the wheel

- speed of implementation
- what customers want
- good integration with back-office systems
- fulfilment.

There are also new processes and roles within the business to get your head around.

When websites were first launched the role of a webmaster was created to ensure that the site ran well and that additions and comments were dealt with. Now, because so many sites have considerable amounts of content, the role is largely taken by an editor – a journalist and wordsmith who can ensure that the content is presented in a readable and accessible manner – rather than a webmaster grounded in the art of technicalities.

Updates and corrections need to be made on a regular basis. There is little that will let a business down more than out-of-date information on the website. In addition, budgeting for anything new is always a tricky problem. Your business should integrate Internet technologies throughout its core business processes. In this there will be costs but there will also be savings.

An intranet reduces the need for re-keying information by flowing transactions and messages automatically. Your budget spreadsheets could be kept on the intranet which will, obviously, have passworded areas to enable the information to be accessed, amended and printed off only by those who are authorised to do so. So everything could be on the intranet – templates, style guides, product information, customers and work in progress, for instance. And if it is all there, but protected by passwords and access arrangements, then there is no reason why anyone who needs to know something within the company cannot find it without disturbing someone else and rummaging through mounds of paper.

By using an intranet a great number of administration-heavy tasks can be reduced and considerable cost saved in the process, not to mention tempers! Order receipts can flow through to order-entry systems that feed the stock control, picking lists and dispatch, whilst replenishing stock used by ordering in new stock. All the accounting procedures likewise can flow through to produce full accounts on an up-to-date basis so that you can see at a glance the current state of the

P&L or how many orders of what magnitude you are getting from a particular source.

Internet-technology-based processes have audit trails just like any good accounting software, but by using e-mail rather than the traditional typed memos you have a dated and timed audit trail of communications too. This is immensely powerful. And, as some companies have found to their cost, it cannot be faked.

Payments on-line need to be thought through very carefully. If you have account-holding customers who normally order by telephone or fax then they can order on-line if you simply ask their advice as to the best way to set up the system for their benefit and usage and then ensure that they are fully aware of the date you go live, how to use the system and what to expect.

Dispatch, shipping and fulfilment are the real killers with e-commerce sites. The infrastructure needs to be in place, tried and tested, before the website goes live. Otherwise disappointed customers will be reluctant to come back to you again. If someone orders on-line today then they expect to receive the goods tomorrow. Leaving the dispatch and fulfilment out of gear with the speed of access and ordering is tantamount to raising customer expectations only to dash them by not delivering fast enough.

> **Essential-e** 'Unless your infrastructure matches your strategy, the system could fall over when you try to deliver. That investment needs to be made up-front – if you don't have the right infrastructure, all that other effort is wasted' (Dave Gill, European MD of F5 Networks).

There are many legal issues that need to be looked into when you are planning an e-commerce venture, including:

- review of any standard terms and conditions/payment terms;
- review of any disclaimers;
- review of contracts with any providers of services relating to the website and any advertisers etc.;
- review of the intellectual property rights used on or in connection with the website, including copyright, trademarks and logos, and in particular a review of any third party licences that are in place or that are required;

- consideration of revenue-share/linking-agreement/click-through issues;
- review of advertising issues in general, including, for example, advertising standards, libel, lotteries/gaming and free gifts or competitions;
- consideration of any licensing requirements, for example consumer credit;
- consideration of any trading-standard issues;
- impacts of jurisdiction of the countries into which you intending to sell.

The E-commerce Directive, which became law on 8 May 2000, has issues that should also be addressed.

With such a lot to do, a well thought out and timely implementation plan is essential, as is a review as you go along. And, as things are moving so fast in the Internet revolution, remember – you might have to change the whole plan in three months! For all that, it won't be long before every business is an Internet business and the Internet is just another business tool.

15

PEOPLE

The set of 10 points that General Electric (GE) followed (see page 96) emphasises how e-commerce demands a change of speed in decision making and implementation of any plans, together with a complete revamp of the mindsets – both corporate and individual. A lot of that will take care of itself if you have strong leadership, a good board and decide that e-commerce should be understood throughout your business.

Changing the way you work is the first indicator that you have begun the process and will also give momentum to the learning curve necessary for the planning and implementation of Internetting your business.

There is a skills shortage of people who know and understand e-commerce as well as business. In fact anyone who has blue-chip experience at a high level together with an understanding of e-commerce and some visionary ideas is well and truly in demand. As with innovation before the age of the Internet, people with a track record in these things are very few at this stage of bubbling Internet implementation.

The cultural divide between the Internet start-ups and that of traditional business is also a discomfiting factor. On top of this, as Christopher Spray of Atlas Venture, the venture capitalist has said, 'Entrepreneurs themselves realise that the people needed to grow a business are seldom those who started it.'

So, old-type boards and managers have to learn to get on with Internet and e-commerce people – and vice versa. If you look inside your business and seek out the creative people and the ones who think laterally you may well find that they are the very same who will help your business the most – by envisioning how you can make the best out of e-commerce.

> **Transition stats** At least 96 per cent of companies do not have e-commerce or new media directors (**www.clearcommerce.com**).

Most existing businesses dip their corporate toes in the Internet torrent by tacking on a little bit of Internet technology to see how it goes. Directors are still wary because the bulk of them don't understand the technology or quite what it can do. What GE did was probably the only way to reinvent themselves and share the knowledge within a reasonable time frame.

But there are other considerations. If the Internet changes everything then should we also look at everything? Rather than tweaking some of the business to encompass e-commerce in a half-hearted way, could a re-think of how the company runs altogether be advantageous?

What about the construction of the board? There has long been jockeying for position between different disciplines. Surveys carried out by IT people to see how many boards have an IT director come up with the result that they think not enough IT directors exist. Similar surveys by human resources people report how few HR directors there are. Indeed there is a tendency when you get a gaggle of IT people or HR people or finance people (it doesn't matter which discipline is grouped together) that they refer to their area of specific expertise as 'our industry' in relation to 'the rest of the business' as if they were separate and not interdependent.

Most people think that the managing director is the most important person in the company and that the chairman is just an *éminence grise* who runs the meetings. Some even run a pecking order for the members of the board from the MD down to ... well, it depends what industry you're in!

So is everything fine on the board construction front? And will boards constituted in the same old way be able to exploit the Internet for the best? Or is it just a matter of perception? We think the answer is 'No'.

In fact, no director of a company is any more important than any other director. The business cannot run without the mix of skills that they all bring – indeed, it would be deficient if one of them were missing. So is the sometimes rarefied air of the boardroom too far from the interface and the real world?

As far as the Internet is concerned there have been many commentators who have bemoaned the lack of IT people of suitable calibre for a position on the board – and the head of IT is the most obvious choice, within most companies, to drive the e-commerce plan forward.

> **Transition info** 'Managers we spoke to broadly agree that senior management and board directors now take IT professionals' opinions much more seriously than a few years ago. However, despite IT managers' increasing influence, their contributions are much less valued by senior business people than those of colleagues in other disciplines' (David Shaw, Director, Energis).

A lot of this concern could be to do with a perception of importance and job titles rather than actually getting the company to work cohesively after an holistic view has been taken and a corporate plan and route map drafted. The fact is that e-commerce professionals are harder to find than those with more traditional skills because of the skills shortage in this area – and they need to be nurtured. However, job titles often get in the way of success and it is time that people got happy with themselves by counting what they do rather than what they are called.

It's all part of the topsy-turvy situation that we're in during this Internet-induced transition. Whilst most companies assume that people can simply be bought for money, things have changed since the dot-com bubble popped a little; e-biz professionals seem to be happier working within a traditional business where they will get more time off, a better work/life balance and a regular pay packet, than jumping ship to the nearest dot-com start-up that offers them share options. Some historic reality has hit e-business and put these matters in perspective.

Adaptable reward strategies – in which the whole remuneration package is reviewed – must be devised. The Internet changes everything.

Transition info 'Salaries for the top people in dot coms could be 40 per cent higher than outside and, for everyone else within the company, 15 per cent higher; and there are the stock options too' (Hay Consulting).

A company in transition – at the speed that being on top of the Internet wave demands – needs to review the salary packages throughout the workforce in the light of workload, quality of work, lifestyle, autonomy, social environment and pace of work. Consideration also needs to be given to how people think they are improving their skills and career prospects – both inside and outside working time. In this, a start-up company operating totally in cyberspace lags behind a clicks-and-mortar company because all its share value is potential, and, of course, may all end in tears and be worth nothing.

However this will change because, even in the spring of 2000, research found that fewer than five per cent of companies had a clearly defined e-business strategy that had been communicated to all levels of management. This sounds surprising until it is remembered that the normal behaviour of people is to tend to work on and prioritise the things that they have been responsible for before. So an IT director will quite easily fall into focusing on internal computing projects or supply-chain management or other issues and miss the bigger picture, and the same tendencies will apply to people in other disciplines.

The only way to address this is to teach e-business throughout the company so that enterprise resource planning can be undertaken as a high priority. This is an automatic leveller and its introduction should lead to a greater ability for a company to work together as a viable team. Sounds a utopian ideal, doesn't it? But if it is not achieved then the business will suffer by having problems that will reduce its functional achievements and therefore its margins.

There is a huge threat to traditional markets which means that action, both in planning an effective e-business strategy and getting the right people on board, must be taken urgently. This urgency should not be underestimated.

So, what's in a name and how does it affect how people do their work and relate to customers as well as their colleagues?

Within Scient, which is a leading Internet consultancy, the role that is almost a hybrid of internal public relations with human resources is renamed as the chief morale officer and has a considerably extended remit. The knock-on effect of this is legion. Accommodating the idiosyncrasies of the people in different parts of the world is part of the way of building mutual respect and team spirit without wiping out the culture of the country in which they work. The scope of the job goes way beyond what would normally be regarded as HR. The whole environment in which the work is undertaken is considered: food, time, work space, decor and what you call your fellow workers ('colleagues' is a favourite). There is also a morale officer in the different locations. People are appointed to this role for six months at a time.

Likewise when recruits are being interviewed, six colleagues spend some considerable amount of their work time in conducting one-to-one interviews and assessing the recruit's skills sets and potential. A comfortable and relaxed atmosphere is also achieved as Scient's workforce consists of roughly equal numbers of both sexes.

This is a global company with offices around the world and it wants to retain its staff. It has reduced the rate of churn from around the normal 20–30 per cent found in the IT sector to 11 per cent. It

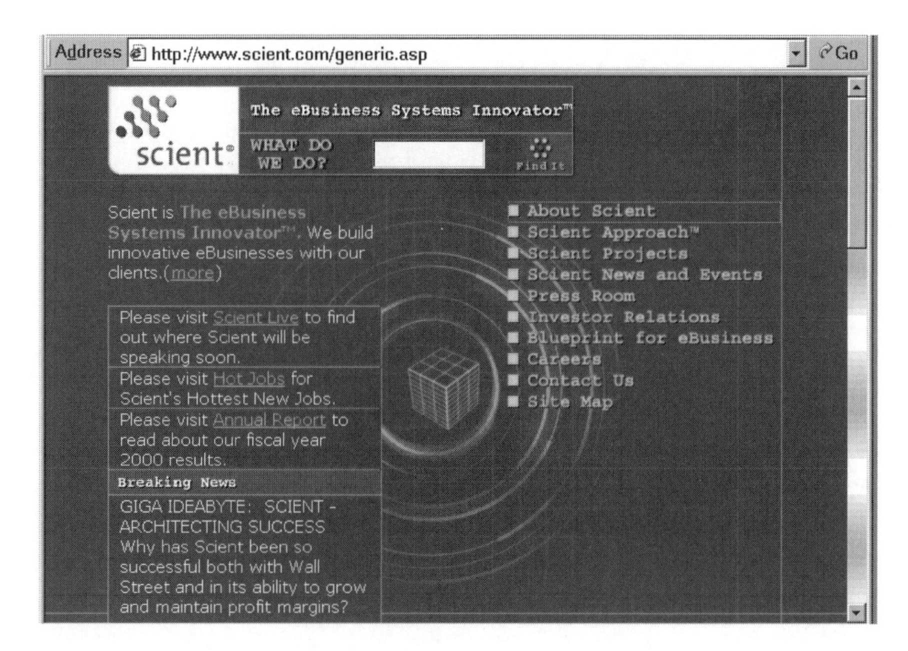

Fig. 15.1 Scient leads the way

cites the costs, both in loss of morale as well as loss of continuity and momentum, as being some of the reasons for its radical move.

In the Internet consultancy world there are many more companies being organised on a similar basis to that adopted by Scient. Presumably their clients will see the business model whilst they work together and it will rub off on the traditional company model. The jockeying for positions by people with specific disciplines is a sad misuse of what a board is for; after all, the multi-disciplinary team that apply themselves to seeing e-commerce projects through to a high level as well as to hard deadlines are, in effect, mini-boards too. A review of the board and its construction is well overdue and could have a dramatically uplifting effect on the way any business runs.

16

WHO'S MINDING THE SHOP?

Have you ever gone to a supermarket looking for a particular product and ended up frustrated because you cannot find it? You ask a shop assistant who directs you to aisle 9, but still you can't see it, and it's as if everyone is ganging up against you to make sure you cannot make the purchase.

Amazingly, there are a great many retail websites that do exactly the same thing. In a survey by e-commerce consultancy Creative Good, dozens of users were put in front of computer screens and asked to test retail sites on the web. In the 10 sites tested – all of them household names – 39 per cent of the users failed to make a purchase because the sites were 'too complicated', whilst 56 per cent of requests made using search engines failed.

> **Quantum shift** Small and medium-sized businesses are under increasing pressure to provide a 24-hour service: 82 per cent now say they operate around the clock (Business Direct, the Co-operative Bank's telephone and internet banking arm).

The lesson is clear. It's all very well spending loads of money on attracting visitors to a website, but if you cannot turn those prospects into sales then you have effectively wasted your money. And don't forget that satisfied customers keep coming back, so not only have you wasted the first-time opportunity of a sale, but all the repeat business as well.

In practice there are very few retail sites that don't have some kind of obstacle to a successful sale. Many require would-be users to battle their way through a succession of minefields, leaving them wondering why they bothered in the process.

One solution is to hand over the entire site to a specialist design company, although this can prove to be an expensive proposition; but then you have to weigh up the advantages of getting a site that works and is user-friendly with one that isn't and doesn't. The old saying that you get what you pay for can be very true in e-commerce.

Another approach is to use one of the many flat-pack shop products that are springing up all over the place. Most of these, such as Shopcreator, Actinic and InterShop, provide templates into which you drop your product details and then all the back-end stuff like

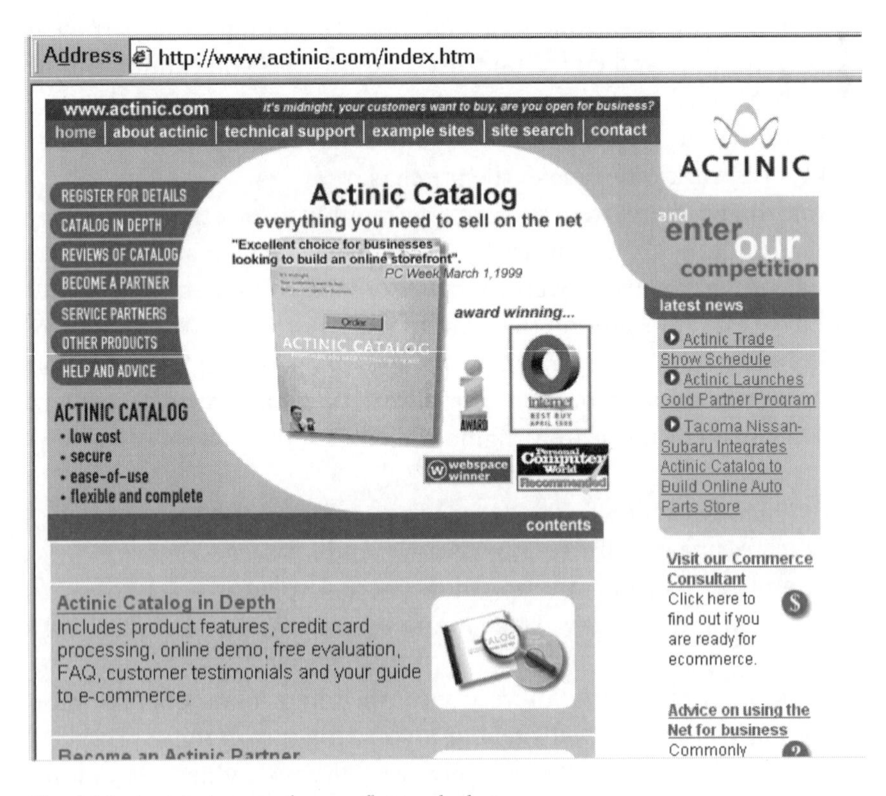

Fig. 16.1 Actinic is one of many flat-pack shops

shopping baskets, secure transactions and credit-card handling are looked after by the software. There are many variations on the type of facilities on offer and the prices vary enormously, with some 'giving away the software for free' and then charging you a percentage of your sales, whilst others charge a fixed fee dependent on how many products you intend to display in your virtual shop.

One of the main problems with the design of on-line stores is that they cannot ever know what proportion of users is going to use which browser, what screen resolutions, what font size settings and so on. It's all very well your techie people using Flash (vector) graphics for fast download, but if the end users don't have a Flash module installed they will see nothing without first having to download a plug-in. Using CSS (style sheets) to determine a fixed font size will only work if the end users have one of the later browser models that supports CSS. Otherwise they could see grossly distorted pages where text and images are all out of alignment. And so it is with JavaScript, dynamic HTML, movie clips and all kinds of other beautiful effects that your website designers might have included in their creation. Tell them to work on the basis that many people still have 28-K modems, don't have such powerful video graphics as they do, and want to get the information that they need fast and easily, rather than be overwhelmed with exciting graphics that take forever to download.

This scenario is most common in on-line shops where there is the propensity to smother everything with huge numbers of graphic files that take forever to download and end by chasing the visitor away. Many people (techies included) seem to have no idea about 'optimising' photographic images, yet an understanding of this is vital for effective transmission of pictures.

Foundations A JPEG image file can be considerably reduced in size by adjusting the amount of compression. For instance, the default setting of most desktop photo scanners is set at 300 dots per inch (dpi), since the majority of desktop printers have a similar resolution. But a computer screen can only resolve densities of around 75 dpi, which means that most images could be compressed considerably before any degradation of the image is visible. The more the compression given, the faster the download of the picture in the visitor's browser.

Apart from the technically challenging pitfalls, there are major problems to be found with ease of use. Retailers often expect far too much of their customers, who have no inside knowledge of how the site has been constructed and therefore can find it difficult to look for the information they want.

For instance, try a little exercise. Say your company is looking for an Internet service provider (ISP) to host its website. You will naturally want to know what services the ISP offers and the price it charges for its offerings. Demon Internet is an ISP that used to top the league table in terms of professionalism and reliability. But when they revamped their website back in 1999 they slipped down the table. Ease of navigation has suffered for the new design and it found searching for information to be rather a struggle. In business terms an ISP is simply a utility.

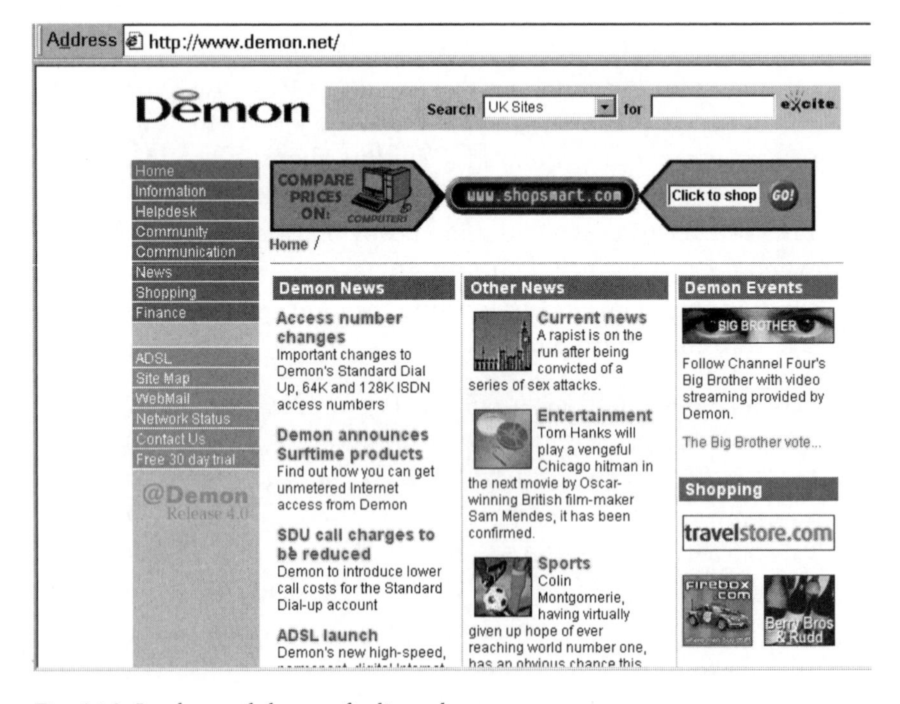

Fig. 16.2 Looks good, but try finding what you *want*

The problem is over familiarity, often by technically minded people who simply do not put themselves in the position of users who do not have a technical background, do not know what special words describe a product or service, and who have no pre-knowledge of how the site has been set up.

Another problem found on many retail sites is that there are further discouragements, such as obscure navigation buttons that appear to lead somewhere totally different from what is expected; items promised that have mysteriously disappeared by the time you have got to the next page; even some sites that ask for credit card details before giving the price of the order. Are they crazy or something? What image does this give of the consistency and management of the business?

Remember that the competition is only a mouse click away, and if you want to generate brand loyalty, you have to ensure customer satisfaction.

According to a report by Shelley Taylor in March 2000 on e-commerce sites:

- 24 per cent do not have a navigation guide for moving around the site;
- 24 per cent do not provide assistance prior to purchase;
- 32 per cent do not give instructions on how to pay;
- only 30 per cent provide information on the product that is to be purchased;
- Only 8 per cent clearly list the products that have been added to a shopping basket.

By anyone's standards, this is a terrible indictment of retail site owners. (And before you sit back smugly, when was the last time you thought about the navigation of your website? Try asking some friends how they found the experience, and be ready to make some immediate changes!)

Of course, we have just been scratching the surface so far. And perhaps we have been a bit premature. For before you can even begin to query the workings of a website, you have to ask yourself that most fundamental of questions – is your retail business actually ripe for placing on the Internet? Ask the following questions:

- How much can be done by mail order?
- How will you deliver the product or service to the end user?
- How reliable is your delivery mechanism?
- How fast can you handle payments?
- How secure are the payments?
- What mechanisms can you put in place to handle queries or customer complaints?
- How will a website affect your cash flow?
- How much will your on-line presence affect your traditional business?

These are all important questions to consider and should be repeatedly borne in mind when designing or commissioning your e-commerce site.

Transition stats An estimated 80 per cent of on-line retailers fail to meet basic customer service standards and have no guarantee of security. They also have a poor returned-goods policy and their delivery times are very unsatisfactory (**www.trusto-on-line.com**).

Take The Body Shop, for instance. This well-known brand of cosmetics and toiletries has been building on a successful mail-order business and delivering products to customers successfully for over three years. By investing heavily in the infrastructure to fulfil on-line orders, as well as the traditional mail orders, it plans to grow Body Shop Direct from a turnover of £20 million in 2000 to £50 million by 2005; and on-line shopping as a percentage of retail sales is projected to be three per cent by 2005 and 10 per cent by 2010.

The main problem The Body Shop may have on its hands is persuading its franchisees (based in 44 countries) that the Internet could complement their businesses and not threaten them by taking customers away from their traditional home markets. The way round this would probably be to use the existing franchises as distribution bases in their home territories so they had a slice of any on-line action.

Fig. 16.3 The Body Shop's UK on-line presence

The reason everyone quotes Amazon as a paragon of e-commerce rectitude is that it looks after its customers and delivers its products in a timely manner and in good condition. The distribution chain is vital to the success of any e-commerce operation. Ignore it at your peril.

17

UP AGAINST THE LAW

They say there are always two sides to every argument, and when it comes to retailing over the Internet, that is no exception.

The problem for the poor e-commerce entrepreneur is that if your customers are upset for any reason with the way they have been treated by your firm, they can simply go play elsewhere. No longer are they held captive because there is nowhere else for them to buy their object of desire. If you cannot supply it in a simple, cost-efficient and timely manner there are plenty of others who will be waiting in the wings to pick up the ball and run with it.

For those who are willing to face the music, there are plenty of legal minefields that have to be avoided to ensure you don't fall foul of Internet law. What you can say, whose content you can use, how you manage your customers ... it seems nowhere is safe from the prying eyes of the legal eagles just waiting to pounce. Just because old laws that were written for paper publishing haven't been tested in an on-line environment doesn't mean you can ignore them with impunity.

Demon Internet found to its cost that items put up by its customers on websites or newsgroups rendered it liable to being sued for libel. When a lecturer, Laurence Godfrey, demanded that Demon remove postings in a newsgroup that Demon hosted, the ISP argued that it couldn't be held responsible, any more than could BT if someone made a slanderous remark over its phone lines. But the judge disagreed and Demon finally settled out of court by paying Dr Godfrey £15,000 together with his costs.

In Germany AOL was found guilty of music piracy on its websites because the service was being used to exchange music files digitally and thereby contravened copyright law.

What is clear is that you need to be very careful indeed if your website gives visitors the opportunity to interact with it in any way. For instance, if your e-commerce site features a chat room or a guest book, or somewhere that comments can be posted, then it is feasible that you could find yourself in the same position as AOL or Demon. And what if you refer someone to another site where they use a free e-mail service to send pirated music files? Could you be liable for what they did?

The American horror novelist, Stephen King, thought up a new method of interaction on his web site **www.stephenking.com**. He posts up the chapter of a book once a month on to this site and requests that those who want to carry on reading it send him a dollar for the privilege. Every month he will post another chapter and

Fig. 17.1 Stephen King has planted the seed

charge another dollar but, unless 75 per cent of those who log on pay up, the book will stop there. (On the first day of publication, 'only' 41,000 downloads took place.)

This is a novel extension of the pay-per-view principle. However, there is no way the readers know how much they will be letting themselves in for in payment, as no one yet knows how many chapters there will be. And what happens to the honest readers who send in their dollars, only to find that more than a quarter of the other readers don't pay up? Will they get a rebate? Unless he has carefully considered all his legal minefields, it could be that Mr King will eventually be attacked by America's notoriously litigious society.

Ground breaker Freenet, the software that allows digital music downloads, is setting up Uprizer, a company designed directly to challenge existing copyright laws. Ian Clarke, its founder, says 'We intend to stay vigorously on the right side of the law' and cites Stephen King's example as the way around the problem of rewarding artists for music.

Take the tricky area of trademarks, for instance. By definition, a trademark can be anything that distinguishes one company's products from that of another. But companies with the same name can be registered in different territories or different markets where product categories are totally unrelated.

Some Web design companies have fallen foul of trademark law by incorporating brand names into their meta tags (the little 'flags' that the HTML code contains in order to attract search engines to the site). Some words such as 'Hoover' and 'Biro' are now used so commonly in everyday language that they can easily slip in unobserved, waiting for an eagle-eyed lawyer to issue proceedings. (In reality, however, a warning letter from the company owning the trademark is normally enough to scare off the trademark predator and get them to remove the offending word.)

Patents can also present problems for e-commerce sites. There is the now-famous case of Amazon successfully suing its arch rival Barnes & Noble in December 1999 when the latter used 'one-click' ordering on its website. The feature was developed by Amazon to

Fig. 17.2 Barnes & Noble, who were successfully sued by Amazon, for use of their patented 'one-click' ordering system

help its returning customers use just one button to paste their credit card and delivery details into a form for their next order.

Perhaps the biggest threat to anyone who deals with any customers (i.e. the entire e-commerce community) is the way in which it handles personal data on individuals.

The UK's first data protection act was passed in 1984, well before e-commerce had made its mark in today's cyber-oriented society. It was set up to protect people from abuses of personal data stored in computer files, but anyone who collects data from individuals needs to notify the data registrar of their activities, unless they are purely for a core internal business process such as staff administration, keeping accounts etc. An e-mail address, for instance, could well count as personal data since it might be able to identify who the sender/recipient was and the firm for which they worked.

The use of cookies (text files deposited on your computer's hard disk as identifiers) to track where visitors are going on your site and which advertisements they are looking at is common on the Web. If you are tracking visitors purely for your own marketing intelligence, then you don't need to inform the registrar; but if you intend – even at a later date – to use the personal data for any reason, then you do.

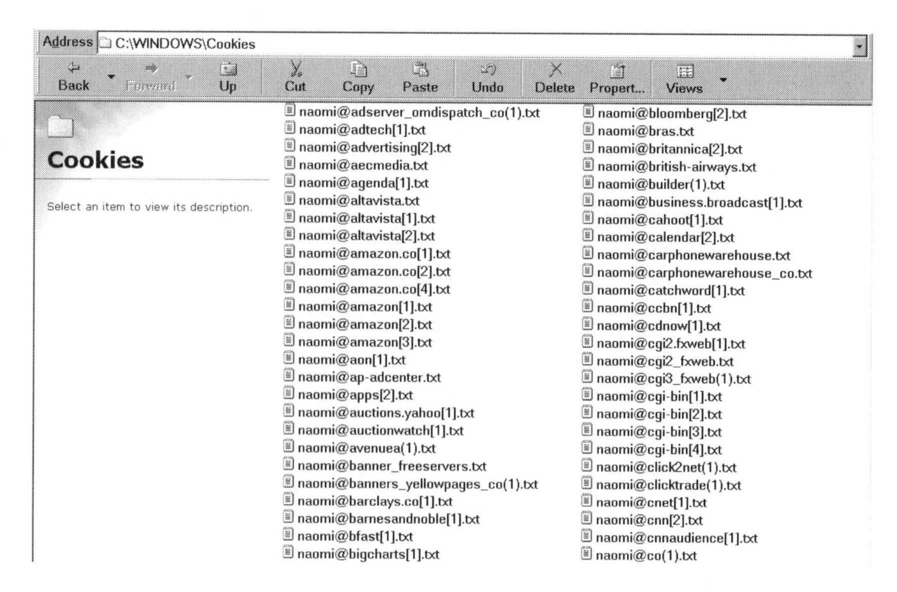

Fig. 17.3 Naomi's cookies won't make you fat!

Although we have been talking here of the UK data protection rules, the fact is that the Internet is by its very nature worldwide; that means that rules that say that personal data is prohibited from being sent outside the EU effectively stop any personal data being posted on the Web without authorisation. (All except personal homepages, of course, since by their very nature they are authorised by the person who put them up.)

Copyright is another issue that covers almost everything on the Internet. Designs, pictures, cartoons, music – whoever created the content has exclusive right to control how it is used unless the copyright is passed to someone else. So if you are commissioning an outside agency to create an e-commerce site for you, make sure you specify in the contract if you want the copyright passed to your firm.

The terms and conditions of your e-commerce business that are posted on your site can also fall foul of international law. For instance, in Germany it is illegal to describe a special offer as 'two for the price of one', as are comparative pricing models. In France, it is illegal to have a commercial site hosted on a French server unless the content is in French. The French even outlaw their citizens from posting bids to auction sites unless the site complies in every respect with French law.

Site lines There are plenty of website checklists on the Internet that you can use to jog your memory and check whether you are breaking the law on content, links, the misuse of data and business terms and conditions. Check out the website of the Association of E-business Professionals (**http://www.e-biz-pro.org/**) for a taster of what's around.

If your e-commerce site is successful you may well find that it pays to allow others to advertise on your site through banner ads. Do remember, though, that you must ensure that your business is protected from any potential liabilities that may arise. If your advertiser is breaching copyright, trademarks or advertising standards, then you might be liable ... unless you have first obtained an indemnity from the advertiser specifically relating to these issues. Even then, an indemnity is only as good as the person giving it. If they go bankrupt, for instance, you will still be liable for their content, and their infringements could well cost you dear.

If you are considering hosting advertising on your site, a good place to go to for advice is the website of the Advertising Standards Authority who publish their codes of practice at **www.asa.org.uk**.

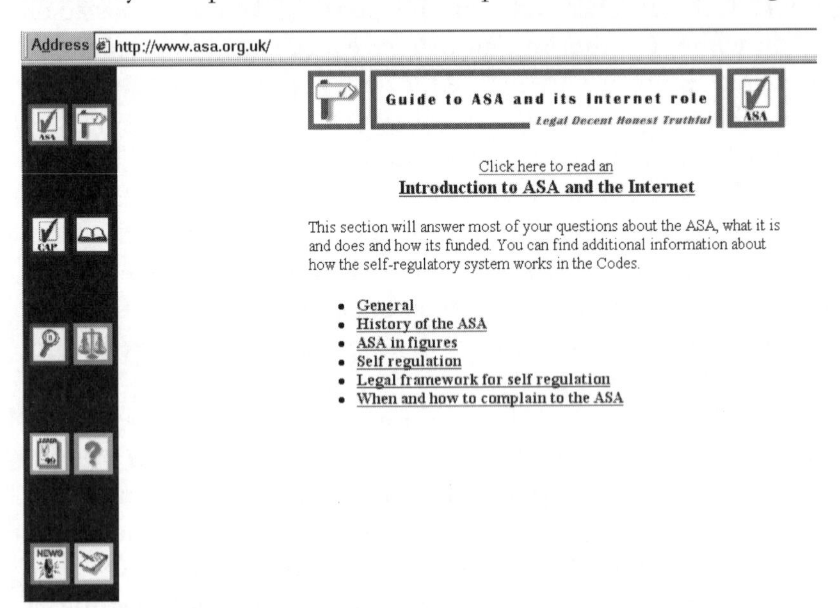

Fig. 17.4 The ASA offers plenty of advice on advertising standards

18

SECURITY AND RISKS

On-line fraud is as old as the Internet itself. Tales abound of hackers getting into corporate websites – usually with a view to leaving a calling card such as a piece of electronic graffiti to show off to their friends that they have breached someone else's security.

Don't you just love it! On-line fraud is a myth and there are more pressing concerns to keep you awake at night – such as a meteor crashing through the roof and setting your bed on fire! (*The Mirror*, August 2000).

A survey by on-line insurers Clickforcover found that six out of 10 managers of smaller companies said they had not considered insuring against risks involved in taking their businesses on-line, including third-party liability, hacker attacks, credit-card fraud and extortion.

Yet with more and more websites featuring e-commerce the dangers posed by security breaches become much more of a risk to business. Malicious hackers can not only deface a site in some way or other, but could obtain and distribute confidential information about customers, or fraudulently obtain goods, or pass themselves off as genuine customers. It hardly bears thinking about!

Just as with the different levels of risk, there are various ways to tackle e-commerce fraud. The first stage in calculating the amount of protection your site requires is to carry out a full Internet audit to

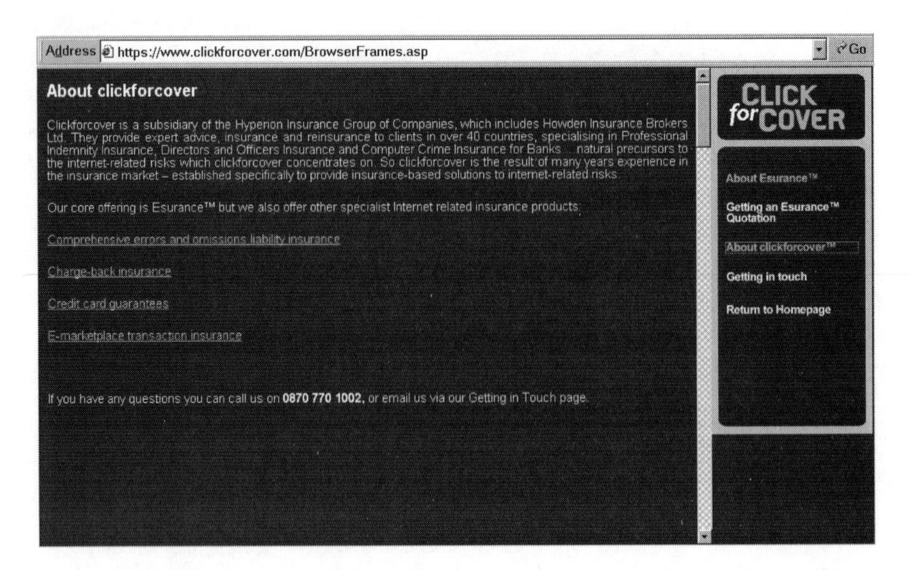

Fig. 18.1 Clickforcover offers insurance for on-line risks

> **Who'd have thought it?** Most fraudulent transactions on the Net appear to be based in dollars and sourced to porn sites. One porn site in particular was infamous for changing the system files on the visitor's computer so that after the first visit the computer would dial into the Web via an international gateway somewhere in eastern Europe without the user's knowledge, thereby generating huge phone bills, a proportion of which was 'earned' by the site.

identify clearly the functionality and reporting facilities required of your site. Based on this intelligence, suitable solutions can be drawn up. There are plenty of standard methods used for securing websites. At the very least, a firewall can limit the access to back-end servers and stop hackers running amok amongst restricted files.

> **Essential-e** It's always a good idea to keep revisiting sites of manufacturers of software products you use to see if any security problems have been reported with their product offerings. Very often they will post 'patches' designed to overcome any problems reported.

There are basically two types of security measures an e-commerce site needs to consider seriously:

- those that prevent intrusion
- those that allow an audit trail for recovery of lost data.

Whoops! In August 2000 Barclays temporarily shut down its on-line bank, iBanking, after receiving enquiries from users who discovered that when they logged on, they were able to view details of other people's accounts, and could apparently transfer money out of them.

Most common in the first type of security breach– intrusion – is the effect that browser operations can have on your server. For instance, many site designers pass critical information around the site as cookies or in hidden form fields. This easily allows hackers to alter critical data, allowing them to trigger functions that they should not be able to access.

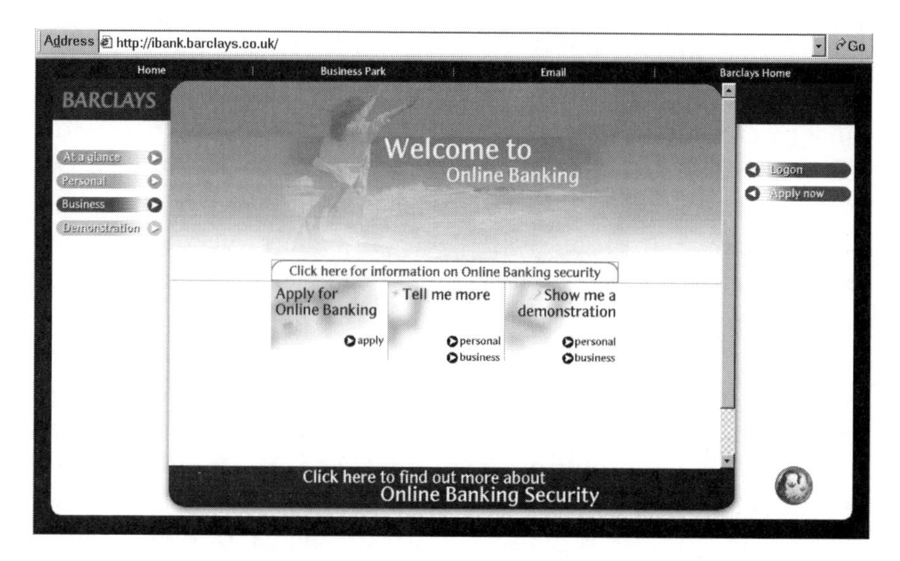

Fig. 18.2 Barclays offers lifestyle banking, but has been rattled by security issues

One way to beat this is to use what are known as 'session cookies', holding all the data pertinent to this transaction at the server side. By logging minimal information, such as the customers' IP (Internet protocol) addresses, a record of the time that transactions took place and a description of the operation performed, basic security can be provided.

You can do other things to flag-up suspected fraudulent transactions. For instance, you could set your server to bring up a warning if a transaction was, say, more than three times the value of an average shopping-cart value; or you could try to detect multiple purchases from one IP address – sometimes a fraudster is able to generate a card number using a software program, and will then try a variety of expiry dates with that card number until one fits. Such a pattern is quite easy to detect and the details can then be passed on to the appropriate authorities.

Whoops! Using a randomly selected credit card number a security guard was able to order goods on a home-shopping channel. This revelation has led to speculation on the repercussions to the world of e-commerce (*Daily Telegraph*, August 2000).

If all these systems appear daunting to you, then you will find that there are plenty of agencies that will look after your site's transactions, including providing the security keys necessary as well as handling the credit-card transactions.

Transactional audit trails are necessary in the realms of business-to-business e-commerce, but although the early adoption of SSL (secure sockets layer) encryption offered some protection it is not really adequate. Instead, something known as PKI (public key infrastructure) needs to be implemented.

Within an e-business environment, it is essential for businesses to be able to identify themselves to one another prior to any type of transaction. It is also necessary to validate sources of information and data, both to confirm their origin and also to ensure they haven't been tampered with on their route over the public network of the Web. In the traditional business model this has always been provided by the physical signing of a piece of paper. In an e-commerce environment, digital signatures provide the same level of protection. In this environment, if the contents of a digitally signed document have been changed, the electronic signature will fail, thereby alerting the recipient that something is wrong or that the content is invalid.

Business transactions also need to be confidential, and this places the need to encrypt the information within a document. PKI achieves all of this by matching a pair of encryption and decryption keys, each one manipulating the data in such a way that you need the reverse key in order to be able to decipher them. Whilst a public key is made available to everyone, a private key is only given out to the user and is otherwise entirely confidential. By using these keys, the identity of a third party can be assured. And by using a digital certificate, issued by a third party such as a bank, its holder can be authenticated. These can be used for establishing secure Internet connections, Web–client authentication, encrypting and signing secure e-mails.

> **Foundations** Key players in the field of PKI include Verisign (**www.verisign.com**), RSA Security (**www.rsasecurity.com**), Baltimore Technologies (**www.baltimore.com**), and iD2 (**www.id2tech.com**).

It might appear that PKI will provide the solutions to all your security problems. Not so, according to a security analyst firm Counterpane, which has published a report on its website at **www.counterpane.com** that claims that PKI is over-hyped. And research by IDC in December 1999 concluded that PKI is still very much in its infancy. In fact, the only countries where PKI has really taken off are the Nordic countries of Finland, Sweden and Norway – perhaps because they already carry ID cards to prove their identity, and so there isn't such a barrier to its public acceptance.

Certainly, concerns are growing in the UK that the adoption of online identity verification could be hindered by the pro-privacy lobby, which argues that authentication infringes an individual's right to privacy. According to Forrester Research in July 2000, the central issue in the debate is giving users a choice over whether to identify themselves or not.

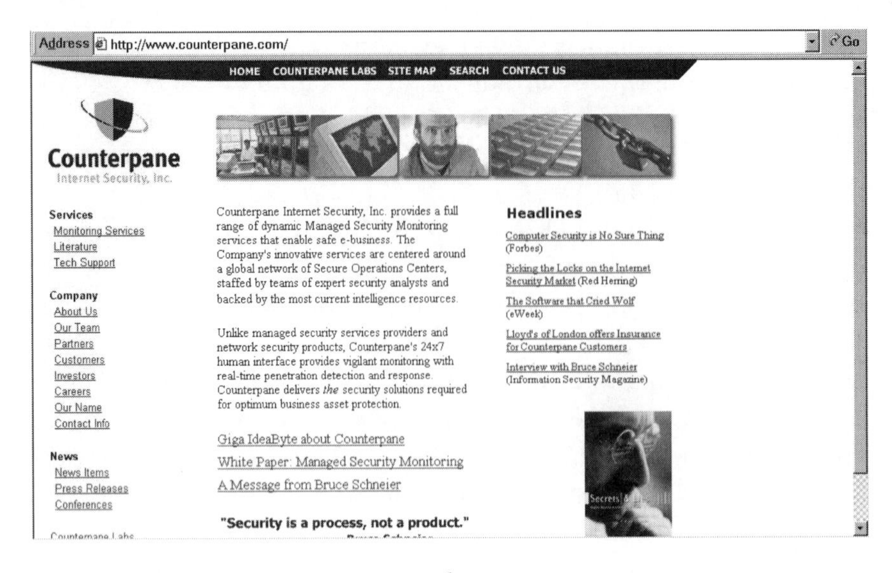

Fig. 18.3 Counterpane comments on on-line security

> **Who'd have thought it?** Some banks are reporting a new phenomenon in reported credit card crime – that of spouse denial. Men, in particular, who have been caught by their partners surfing around sex sites, are increasingly claiming fraudulent use of their credit card numbers when the credit card bill arrives at the end of the month. If only they knew that the Internet leaves a trail of sites visited splattered across their computers' hard disks, which can prove which sites they have visited, then perhaps they wouldn't be so quick to deny what has been going on!

There was uproar in 1999 when Intel announced that its Pentium III chip contained an electronic tag unique to each chip, which could be read over the Internet. It was designed to let IT managers track computers within a firm and administer them remotely, but Intel was forced to release the chip with the feature switched off by default.

Eventually digital cash could be the answer to e-security, since there is no need for transactions to be linked to the buyer, just as in the real world where we can pay by cash and so remain anonymous. Time will tell.

19

MARKETING, DESIGN AND BRANDING

On the Net, marketing, design and branding need a new mindset because all the business rules have changed. Tried and tested methodologies and measurement in the world prior to the Internet simply don't work.

Too bold a statement? Well, when websites were first put up, for instance, advertising was cited as a good potential income stream to the site owner. Would-be advertisers would rush to the new potential money spinner, lured by assured declarations of the number of 'hits' on a site. These made site traffic sound astronomically high and the potential to get an advertisement in front of such an apparently large audience made the advertising gurus salivate.

Or did it? It turned out that 'hits' were not all they were cracked up to be, and advertising as a form of revenue on a website now forms only a small part of the income stream for most sites.

Transition info 'Hits' on a website are calculated not by the number of visitors, but by the number of graphics and hyperlinks on a page that are visited. So, if you look at a Web page and it has six click buttons for navigation then you have six graphics for the buttons as well as six hyperlinks, making 12 'hits' so far. Add to that any graphics that are on the page, say another 10, and you have a total number of 'hits' of 22.

> (We won't complicate matters by identifying graphics that are split into slices because of their size.) There is no qualitative assessment of these, nor is there any quantitative assessment as to whether the visitor actually wanted to see your site in the first place.

Therefore, the number of hits tells you very little and advertising revenues have fallen dramatically since the market leaders finally tumbled to this fact.

Advertising costs and benefits have long been measured by identifying the numbers of a publication produced or peak viewing times and audiences. Now on-line advertising is looking for reliable information on audience measurement, in order to arrive at a pricing structure and assess the cost–benefit analysis. Since audit trails, clicks and balances can be recorded and instantaneously tracked on the Internet, it was assumed that data recording traffic would be easy to produce, showing precisely how many people had viewed the advertisements.

Not so. The opposite has happened. Claims were made for 'hits' showing the huge numbers of people visiting sites and when this, obviously erroneous, method of counting traffic was shown to be wrong, the balloon of on-line advertising sales finally popped. The difficulty in tracking and measuring on-line audiences has turned out to be a huge block to the growth of advertising on the Internet. Advertisers repeatedly state that they have to keep out of Internet advertising because audience measurements are not good enough to justify their moving in.

So we find tracking and process, those old chestnuts, have halted the predicted exponential growth of on-line advertising, and in its wake scuppered many a dot com's aspirations of megadosh when advertising revenues formed a large part of their income streams. We have ended up with a form of stalemate. Advertisers are trying to build momentum because they need that to diversify their businesses across the different media and platforms. Meanwhile, Web publishers are working on different business models that don't rely so heavily on advertising.

The plot gets thicker. Technology is offering opportunities with one hand and flattening them with the other. For instance, for advertisements to be effective on the Web, advertisers are dependent upon fresh downloads when a regular visitor revisits a site. However, this is not always going to happen because so much is kept in the cache of a browser to enable faster repeat downloads and many set their browser not to 'waste' time downloading the same pages again. So unless visitors can be persuaded to set their browsers to reload pages every time they log on and 'refresh' their download when they view a site again, then the new advertisement will not be seen.

This dilemma gave someone else the opportunity to develop software that would bust the caching system, and that led to someone else developing the cache-buster-buster, and so on – round and round but getting not very far. There are also those people working on advertisement aborting software that can wipe the advertisements from your viewing – not a good thing for the admen.

Who'd have thought it? A brochure from Elderstreet Investments (a venture capital firm) contains a useful insight into the Internet, claiming it is 'God's way of taking money from VCs [venture capitalists] and giving it to advertising agencies' (*The Sunday Times*, July 2000).

Measuring became more of an exact science when selective traffic tracking identified a visitor as a viewer of a particular advertisement when they clicked on the advertisement. This, of course, blew away all the previously agreed measurement criteria for advertising that applied, say, to a newspaper. Readership and distribution had always been regarded as enough, even though no proof could ever be found of the numbers of readers who actually read an advertisement in a newspaper – unless, comparing like with like, you only count the numbers of people who respond to the advertisement. The figures on which revenues were based for many years would have to be thrown out.

In the end, the various anomalies will all be accepted as part of the compromise necessary in order to quantify the costs and benefits of advertising on the Web. But for the moment there are many different thoughts on the validity of measurements and imprecision in number crunching – which leaves the whole thing nicely confusing.

Having got the admen into a kerfuffle the Internet has also confused branding.

Fig. 19.1 One of Lastminute's brilliantly topical (but cheeky) ads brings a smile and builds the brand

On the Internet, branding must be crystal clear to the public. Here, public relations (PR) is probably the most powerful tool that Internet companies can harness. Branding, like all marketing, needs to be well thought out to be effective. And as more and more Internet companies start up it becomes more and more difficult to look different and be noticed. Identifying and really honing in on a unique selling point (USP) for a company or product is essential to enable it to be spotted above the crowd.

Old brands carry baggage with them. Singer, in most people's minds, meant sewing machines – reliable sewing machines; Hoover was synonymous with vacuum cleaners that are the best; Rolls Royce meant the best and most expensive engines, which sat in the best and most exclusive cars; and Coca-Cola ... well, Coca-Cola surpasses all in being a totally universal brand.

Since the age of the Internet there has been a tendency to launch products (or companies) using off-the-wall names or names which are totally descriptive of what the company does. So, Lastminute.com explains exactly what it does and how to get to it – whether it fulfils its promise is entirely beside the point. Amazon on the other hand doesn't say anything about what it does, but it built the brand that

Fig. 19.2 Coca-Cola maintains its brand on-line

will keep it in the forefront of Internet history as being a big spender on infrastructure and as being one of the great Internet pioneers.

> **Milestones** Rock band Jethro Tull have won the right to the Internet address Jethro-Tull.com after it was decided that another had registered the name in bad faith. Tull have succeeded where Sting failed, after it was decided that sting is actually 'a common English word' (the *Guardian*, August 2000).

So it is a matter of identifying the target market and getting something to focus on that which will enable a brand to be picked up and accepted. Clarity of message, a brand that is easy on the tongue, and the fulfilment of promise when the site is tested are essential components for the word-of-mouth building that will come. In choosing the name Egg, the Prudential made it easy for new users to remember the product and the site. Its wackiness appealed to the younger public, who were the target market.

Fig. 19.3 Who'd have thought you could buy bras from a finance house?

After all, technology and all its complications are not easy to explain, so an easy concept, followed by an easy and beneficial product line, led to a golden Egg for Prudential – until the me-too products from Abbey and Halifax came along and attempted to crack its shell.

In your terrestrial business, continuity of marketing image on all your company literature, business cards, headed paper and so on is essential. This branding and continuity should also be reflected in your Web presence. The baggage that comes with the service and products you supply, such as 24-hour turnaround or an 'everyone should have one' product, must also be reflected in the website – but without losing the flexibility and fun of the genre. The Internet is interactive whereas company literature is not, so a different attitude and attributes need to be applied to the preparation of the brief and specification of the Web presence.

Figuring out who your target markets are is the first priority before commissioning masses of literature or devising and implementing a marketing campaign. Target markets all behave differently in relation to the Internet. However, you can target very narrowly defined groups and niche markets if you plan it right. And to maintain the interest in a website, promotions are often a way of getting people back to visit again.

> **'Twas ever thus:** According to an Amazon.co.uk survey in the summer of 2000, Lara Croft was more widely recognised by young adults than Gordon Brown, and Pikachu was more familiar to 16–21 year-olds than was Tony Blair.

Harvesting databases can be a very lucrative and cost-saving way of ensuring that you address the right potential customers with the right products and services. You can, for instance, capture data from people who come to your site and therefore make the targeting of marketing messages more specific to individuals. However, before you attempt to address this you should follow these six golden thoughts which can save you money, time and frustration:

1. Your business objective must be clear.
2. It is best to talk to the people who will use the data – guessing what they want to do with it won't help.
3. It may be better to get survey experts or consultants in who specialise in statistics.
4. Find the flexible data warehouse system you really need.
5. Work out how the data will change over the period in which you are intending to capture it.
6. Don't forget that helpdesks and other services may well need to be added and this cost must be factored in to the budget.

PART 4

BLUE SKIES

20

FOCUS ON THE FUTURE

Do you have a wedding anniversary coming up? If so, why not suggest to your partner a romantic weekend ... in Helsinki?

The fact that Helsinki was designated European City of Culture for the year 2000 has nothing to do with it – but does have everything to do with IT. Anyone who is serious about the future direction of e-commerce could do a lot worse than experience the Finnish way of life where the rate of Internet users per head of population is higher than anywhere else in the world.

> **Transition info** Linus Torvalds, the man behind the operating system Linux, is Finnish; the Internet relay channel (IRC) was developed in Finland; anonymous servers were developed in Finland; and phone costs – both mobile and fixed – are amongst the lowest in the world, thanks to there being some 45 different phone companies in competition with one another.

When you arrive at Helsinki airport, make sure you rent a mobile phone straight away; then when you find you haven't any spare change for a soft drink you won't need to worry because all you need do is telephone the Pepsi machine over in the corner and it will deliver a plastic bottle into the dispenser. The cost will be added to your phone bill, with a 17 per cent surcharge to pay for the administration.

No change to practise your strokes on a golf range? Use your mobile. Want your car washed? Use your mobile. Need something copied in a copy centre? Use your mobile ... You get the idea!

Transition stats Finland has 5.16 million people, 1.5 million saunas and 3.3 million mobile phones used by two in three Finns.

Finland is so wired that you'll need to watch out if you decide to speed down Helsinki's roads. Well, you would if you lived in Finland, anyway. The police officers who catch speeding motorists dial up from the roadside to the federal tax ministry computers to check a driver's income. The amount you are fined is determined by your level of income, and claiming poverty to these agents of law and order simply won't wash in a land where the tax authorities know better.

A project called Helsinki Arena 2000 plans to map all the 24,000 square kilometres encompassing greater Helsinki; when it is complete, residents will be able to call up the map on their PC or mobile phone. So you won't have any excuse for getting lost. You'll also be

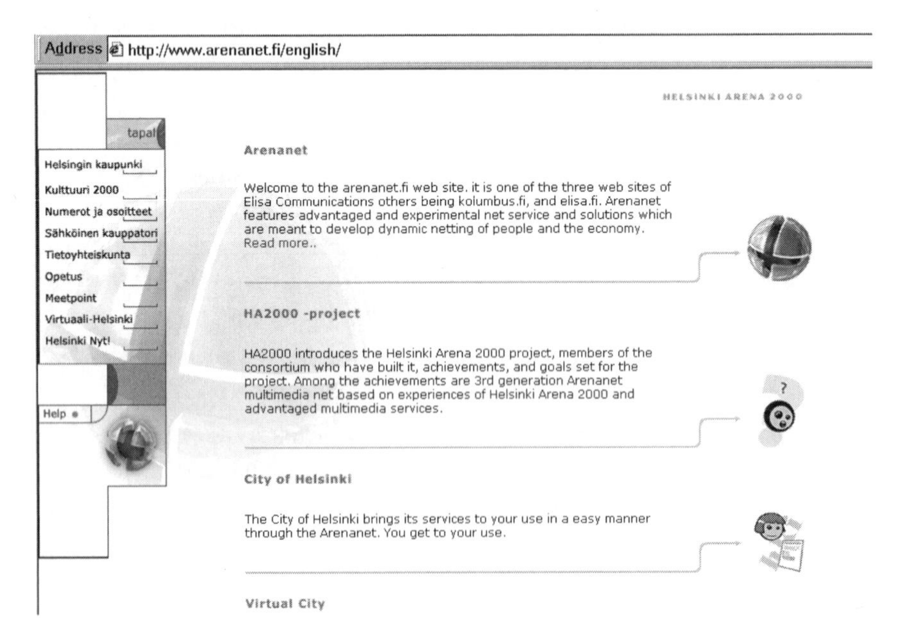

Fig. 20.1 The Helsinki Arena 2000 project is in its development stage

able to find the nearest fast food outlet, or when the next bus is arriving. So you won't have an excuse for arriving late at an appointment, either. Helsinki Arena 2000 will also provide true multi-cast video conferencing and a whole lot more besides.

> **Transition stats** In 1999 Finnish mobile phone users sent some 500 million short text messages, averaging 50 per cent of their phone bills.

And that's what's going to happen in the UK and the rest of mainland Europe very shortly. WAP (wireless application protocol) allows you to browse the Web, get e-mails from your mobile, e-mail to a fax machine, e-mail to voice, and much, much more. Recently Amazon launched Amazon Anywhere, allowing customers to shop from their phones without making a voice call; customers simply order their book using the keypad.

WAP will also allow workers in the field to communicate in a much more sophisticated way with HQ than has been possible up until now, simply by plugging in portable computers to a modem on a portable phone. Meanwhile, Waitrose claims to be the first supermarket to sell goods over WAP; and Virgin Radio is the world's first

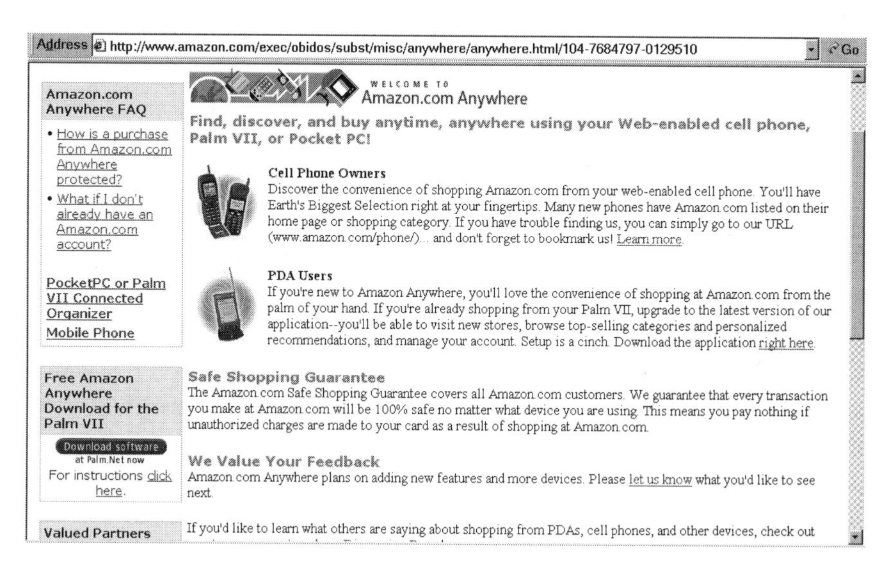

Fig. 20.2 Amazon Anywhere lets you buy books over your WAP phone

interactive radio service using WAP (your mobile shows the names of the records being played and allows you to buy the music on-line.)

Yet there was much over-hype when WAP phones first made their appearance at the turn of the century. Connections were extremely slow, displays were very small, and in black and white and mainly text-based at that. The first implementation of WAP has left a sour taste in the mouth for those technophiles who rushed off to buy a WAP-enabled phone. And sending e-mails – another WAP feature – is tedious on traditional mobile phone handsets, so manufacturers are struggling with putting decent keypads on to these mobile devices.

So why the excitement? Well, the convergence of the Internet and the growth of the mobile phone market is seen by many as the key to the future, with predictions that mobile access to the Internet will outstrip fixed access within the next few years.

Foundations The Woolwich Building Society claimed a first when it opened a WAP channel in August 1999 for its Open Plan account holders, allowing them to check balances, make transfers and pay bills.

The real fun time will begin, though, in 2003 when 3G (third generation) access becomes reality, although the arrival of general packet radio services (GPRS) by 2001 will enable permanent connection to the network. Access speeds will rise from around 9 kB/sec in the summer of 2000, to more than 56 kB/sec the following year, 100 kB/sec in 2002 and 2 MB/sec in 2003 – or a 200 times speed increase in three years. With 3G will be full-scale convergence of several existing technologies on a single handset, including telephony, computing and video. It will feature higher bandwidth, faster data speeds and a more flexible radio interface. Nokia believes that in 2003 there will be more mobile phones connected to the Internet than PCs.

Using the global positioning system (GPS) it will also be possible to locate phones to within a few metres, and this will allow new applications to be developed, some of which are not to everyone's liking. For instance, imagine you were walking down London's Oxford Street and you happened to be passing a shoe shop. Now, that shop might have a special sale on, and if data about your buying habits

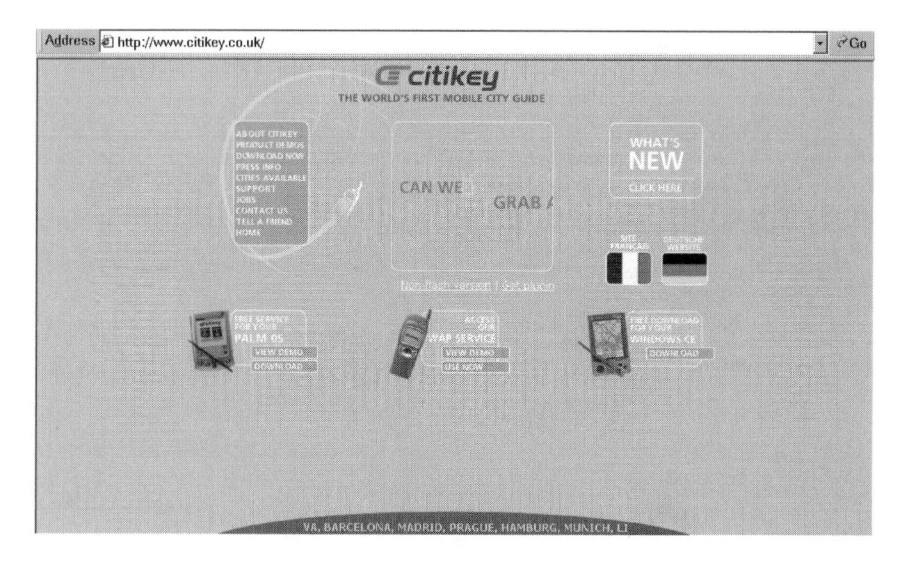

Fig. 20.3 Citikey provides key information on cities worldwide

identified that you were a second Imelda Marcos, it could 'push' an advertising message to your personal mobile inviting you inside to inspect their wares.

Local weather forecasts, train and tube service information, maps and real-time traffic reporting are all ideal for this type of environment; in June 2000, Citikey launched its WAP site in London allowing you to browse listings of restaurants, venues and events. Then there will be real-time parking systems developed which will be able to identify where you are and list available car parks with space nearby, as well as on-street parking.

The relentless push towards a mobile telephonic future is one scenario that most seasoned observers agree upon. Another technology that is also likely to make a major impact on society in the next decade is something called 'Bluetooth'. If you thought mobile telephony was something to shout 'wow' at, then consider this. Experts now expect it to be installed in up to four billion devices by 2005.

Who'd have thought it? Harald Blatand (Bluetooth) was a tenth-century Danish Viking king who is credited with uniting Norway and Denmark and bringing peace and harmony to his kingdom.

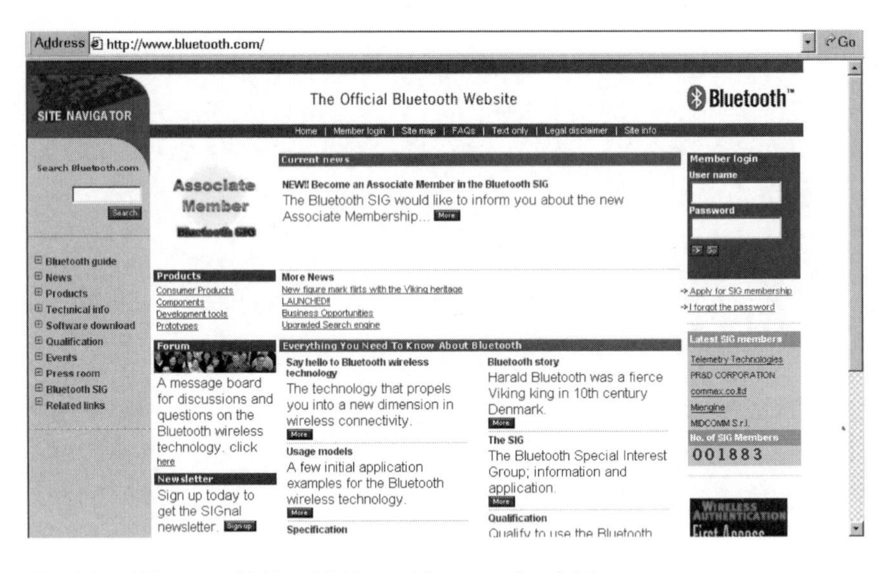

Fig. 20.4 What would Harald Blatand have made of this?

So what is Bluetooth? Simply, a cheap, low-powered technology standard allowing cable-free connections between mobile phones, palmtops, laptops, keyboards and anything else that can be connected by short-range (i.e. up to 10 metres) mobile radio links.

Offices in the future will be cable-free, but Bluetooth will also allow us to use our mobiles as a credit card, a remote control and as a fixed phone. It will also allow us to change video and satellite TV channels from any room in the house so we don't need one system for every room.

Then there are the oft-quoted 'predictions' of the sci-fi brigade who tell us that we will be connecting our fridges or washing machines to the Net. Or add a bar-code reader and you could have your fridge 'read' every item of food removed from its interior and e-mail Tesco Direct (or some other supermarket retailer) once a week automatically requesting further supplies of milk, sliced bread and smoked salmon.

So what of the future? As *Computer Weekly* stated in the spring of 2000, 'mobile devices could soon outsell wristwatches.' The future is wireless connectivity combined with the Internet – which could turn out to be an even bigger money spinner than the Internet itself.

The days of *Thunderbirds* and *Star Trek* are fast becoming reality.

21

FASTER THAN A SPEEDING BULLET

'It's just like swapping your car for a private jet.' So ran a headline in the *Financial Times* in March 2000 when it extolled the benefits of switching to ADSL (asynchronous digital subscriber line) technology.

ADSL technology allows simultaneous phone, fax and high-speed Internet use over the same phone line with connection speeds up to 35 times faster than is obtainable from a traditional 56-K modem. It's not difficult to see the appeal of ADSL for the consumer. For businesses, it is a solution that is finally catching up with one of the biggest problems faced on the Net – that of limited bandwidth and download speeds.

As well as allowing Web pages that download almost instantaneously, you can hear audio in near-CD quality, view video films on demand, enjoy or provide vastly improved interactive shopping, plus high-quality low-cost telephone calls and video conferencing. Initially it will be provided with downstream speeds of 512 kbps, 1 Mbps and 2 Mbps. The lowest rate is deemed by BT to be suitable for small businesses. Those who need video on demand will opt for the faster, more expensive options.

At the time of writing charges for ADSL connections are in the region of £50 per month. Although this might appear very high for individual access accounts, small businesses in particular should

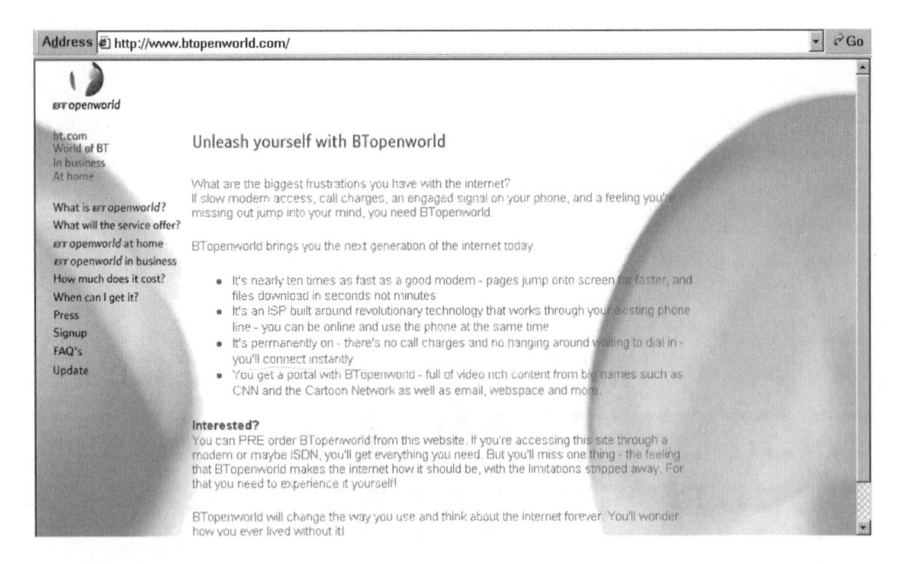

Fig. 21.1 BT openworld neglects to mention the key acronym ADSL

> **Foundations** ADSL works by using radio frequencies sent along the normal copper wires to the telephone node (not always the exchange), allowing broader bandwidth and thereby allowing more data to be transmitted. Because voice frequencies are not used for the data transmission, separate voice calls can be superimposed upon data transfer along the same wires.

appreciate this level of charging when comparing it with traditional lease-line costs which start in the region of £6000 per year. Nevertheless, in America charges start at around £19 a month, and it is not unreasonable to expect the UK charge to fall once BT's local loop monopoly (i.e. for the copper wires that run into your premises) ends in July 2001.

ADSL can only be supported at distances up to around 3 km from the node, so there is likely to be a new community divide between the 'haves' and the 'have-nots' where this technology is concerned. It is something that businesses will have to get their minds around since it is unlikely that in rural areas it will ever be feasible to provide ADSL connections; so if speed of Internet delivery is crucial to the future of your business, you may have to think about relocating some time in the not too distant future.

Or will you? There are other technologies being developed that also offer fast Internet access. An American company called Teledesic, for example, is building a global, broadband 'Internet-in-the-Sky' network which will provide affordable, worldwide, 'fibre-like' access to telecommunications services such as computer networking, broadband Internet access, interactive multimedia and high-quality voice.

Teledesic – which has the backing of Boeing, Bill Gates, Saudi Prince Alwaleed bin Talal and Motorola – will enable broadband connectivity for businesses, schools and individuals anywhere on the planet via 288 low-orbit satellites (which will eliminate the long signal delays normally experienced in satellite communications) and will enable the use of small, low-power user equipment to send and

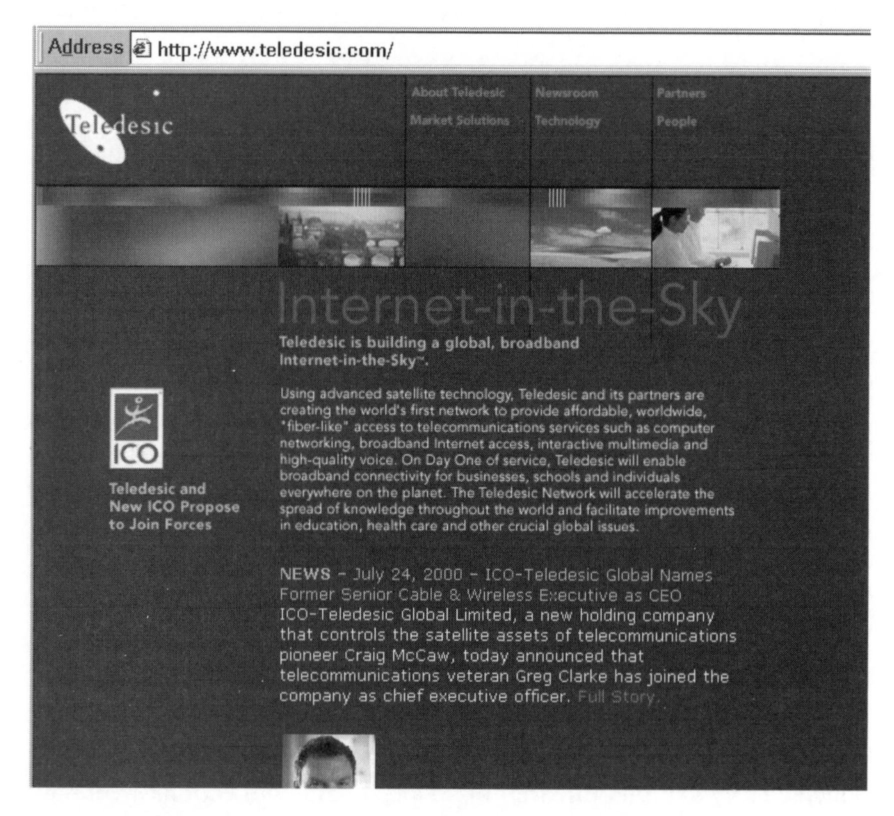

Fig. 21.2 Teledesic – soon to make space the off-world version of the M25?

receive data. The fixed user equipment will mount on a rooftop and connect inside to a computer network or PC. Service is expected to begin in 2004.

Meanwhile, one-way access via satellite has been available for some time through broadcast satellites such as the Easat service that piggy-backs on Eutelsat 13, which is co-located with Hotbird.

Yet another technology, using the powerlines that make up the low-voltage electricity distribution system, offers two-way high-speed access and gets round the problem of 'the last mile' of local copper loop that links users to modern fibre-optic telecommunications networks. PLT (powerline telecommunications technology) could be a perfect route for the UK's regional electricity companies to get a foothold in the telecommunications marketplace. However, technical obstacles such as line noise and transformer interference have hindered its development, although companies such as Siemens, Ericsson, Alcatel and RWE Energie are all pressing ahead with its development.

The race is on Fortunes await the countries and companies that get in early in developing the souped-up successor to the Internet, the Grid, which will deliver computing power in the same way that the National Grid provides electricity (*Financial Times*, August 2000).

And then, of course, there are the cables that have been installed by many a cable TV company across Britain, Europe, the USA and other parts of the world. Many cable TV companies are now adding Internet access through their TV cables, allowing faster connection than has previously been possible with 56-K modems.

There is a growing consensus, however, that broadband wireless access, provided by mobile operators, will eventually be the outright winner, due to its cost efficiency in point-to-multipoint operation and continuous upgrades to its infrastructure. A report from Datacomm Research predicts that the users of high-speed wireless links will outnumber their wireline counterparts by 2004.

Whatever technology your business chooses to adopt, there are a number of initiatives launching 'fat pipes' across Europe and the USA, which clearly demonstrate that high-speed data connections are a high priority for many consumers. Showcase events to highlight the advantages of broadband included the 'webcast' of a live performance of Verdi's *Aida* at the opening night from Verona's Arena. E-Aida suffered from technical problems, however, with the video streaming falling over, although the audio streaming settled down well enough to make listening possible. The techniques of webcasting will be high on the expertise learning list for many companies as webcasting promises a much richer experience than an imitative TV broadcast.

If you are still in the dark as to why you should worry about the arrival of high-speed Internet access, then consider this. The convergence of broadcast and broadband media has been predicted for some time, but now it's actually happening.

EMI's proposed tie-up with Time Warner in December 1999 and Time Warner's subsequent merger with AOL on 10 January 2000 would have created a conglomerate that will dominate the world

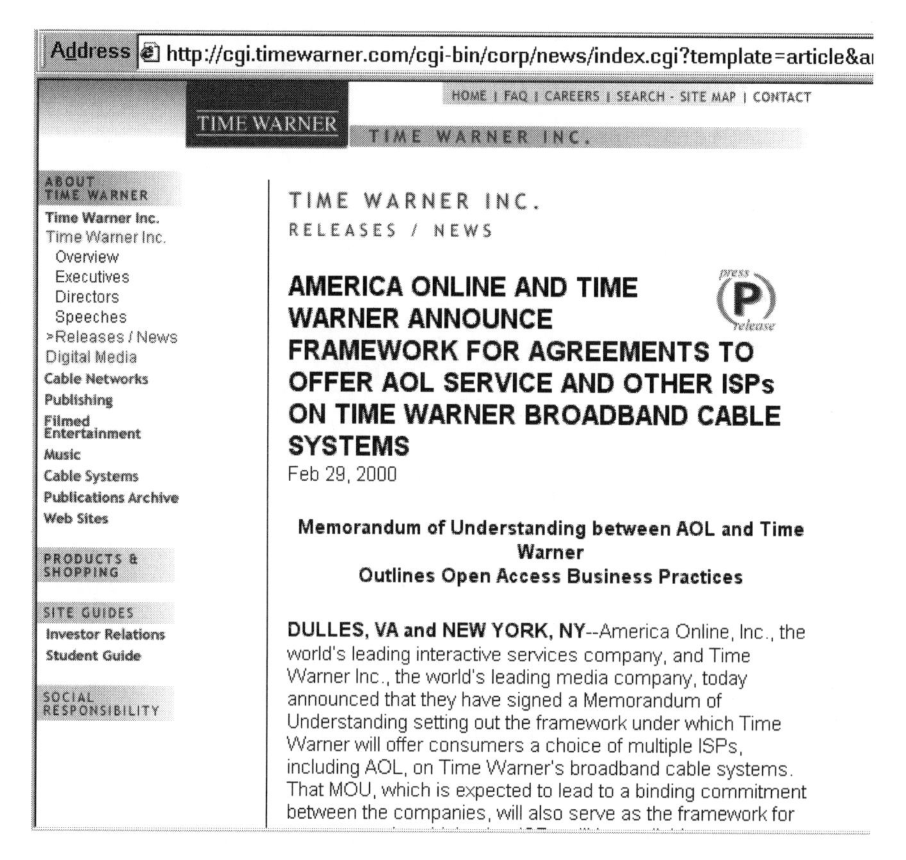

Fig. 21.3 Time Warner and AOL roll out their global plans

media market. If anyone ever doubted the power of the Internet as a commercial medium, then it is high time they thought again.

Just think of it. AOL and Time Warner will between them generate revenues of over $30 billion; they will have a market capitalisation of $350 billion; and they will have a foot in the camps of content, distribution and technology. Effectively the new giant will dominate the entire on-line market.

EMI expects 10 per cent of its sales via the Internet by 2004, and by marrying two million song copyrights with AOL's 23 million subscribers, it seemed a gigantic opportunity. EMI's participation in the Time Warner/AOL venture was, however, prevented by Brussels Eurocrats 9 months after the initial announcement. Time Warner brings CNN cable news to the party, in addition to *Time* magazine and Looney Tunes. AOL also owns Netscape, which now has expanded into areas beyond its original Web browser – for example, to e-commerce software, on-line auctions, on-line payment systems and business-to-business exchanges.

As Time Warner also runs the second biggest US cable operation after AT&T, with more than 10 million subscribers (not to mention its high-speed Internet access over cable via its Road Runner service), AOL/Time Warner amply demonstrates that content is a hugely valuable commodity in the interactive arena.

> **Ground breakers** 'The impressive speed with which the BBC, CNN and the Press Association's websites were able to cover the Concorde crash highlights the multiple platforms now available for accessing and distributing information' (*Financial Times*, August 2000).

So just look at the process changes in that one! While everyone was looking at the awesome power of Microsoft, and taking it to court for its alleged anti-competitive practices, the likes of AOL/Time Warner came charging up from the rear, ready to give a bloody nose to Internet and entertainment companies.

As Andersen Consulting's James Hall told the *Financial Times* in January 2000:

> The new economy is really happening and it is changing what our clients are asking us to do. In the boardroom the greatest

challenge is to understand that the rate of change is so fast that to do nothing is worse than almost anything else you could do.

The convergence of broadcast with broadband media will also open up huge possibilities because of the personalisation that will be possible in the delivery of rich content to end users. In the same way that it is already possible for content sites (such as newspapers and 'e-zines') to provide pages made up 'on-the-fly' that reflect the interests of individual users, so, too, will Web TV companies offer personalised content for their viewers.

Some observers believe that, in the future, digital TV companies may have to make up their minds about whether to concentrate on building a rapport with their viewers, or developing content instead. Setting up interactive services is a very different ball game from delivering straight content, and it could be that having merged broadband with broadcast services, they are once again split into broadcast and narrowcast.

22

SOCIO-ECONOMIC TRENDS AND THE FUTURE ROLE OF GOVERNMENT

The world is changing. Everything that the 'older generation' came to accept as normal is being turned on its head. Nowhere is this more true than in the world of work.

The *éminences grises* in the company hierarchy – the men (usually) over 45 who for so long relied on their secretaries or PAs to work the computers, type the letters and do the filing – are suddenly finding themselves marginalised as computerisation (dynamised by the advent of the Internet) has blurred the edges of who does what as well as where the responsibility and power lie.

The urgency of e-mail requires that the recipient deals with correspondence themself. And that implies a familiarity with basic processes such as filing and keyboard skills. Those who rely on their assistants to print off their e-mails for them to dictate or hand-write a reply to be typed lose out on the efficiencies and advantages of the new medium. The speed of change is so great that it is almost too late for many to catch up. The social upheaval this will cause is alarming many.

For that same group, used to the reverence associated with the size and build of their desks, it is galling to find that size (of desk!) no longer matters; and worse still that 'hot desking' and virtual working make such icons an anachronism in the modern world.

The writing was almost certainly on the wall a decade ago when 'dress-down Fridays' were introduced, first in the USA and then in Britain. Heralded as the beginning of a great revolution in office life, and a key to motivating employees, it turned out to be an idea that was not so brilliant after all. Once employees weren't obliged to dress up for work, it appears they no longer felt compelled to show up either, or if they did, they started behaving as if they were out on the tiles. Flirtatious behaviour was on the increase and companies had to bring in new rules to temper the absence of old ones. It all seems so indubitably obvious now, doesn't it?

But with the advent of computerisation, the Internet and now e-commerce, Pandora's box has opened and – to mix a metaphor – no one is any longer able to squeeze the genie back in the bottle (assuming they wanted to, of course).

For the first time, there is a serious possibility of people having 50-year retirements, or certainly people who could be retired for longer than their working lives. That said, both the Henley Centre and the Employment Policy Institute believe that older workers could become more employable because they are more service-oriented and have better social skills than the 'young upstarts'. These older workers will graduate to the high-street jobs, whilst the Internet will be the stalking ground of the younger generation of workers.

The Henley Centre is predicting a two-tier class structure: skilled workers who will include consultants and gurus in their particular fields; and a servant underclass who will do the manual jobs to save time for the skilled workers.

The remote Internet model of working doesn't suit everyone, however. Many companies that tried working remotely on the tele-working model and interacting with one another over e-mail and in chat rooms found that this way of working lacked the personal element and people weren't able to bounce ideas off one another so easily. The myth of remote working taking over from office environments is likely to go the same way as that hoary old chestnut, the 'paperless office'.

The age of e-commerce may well be a 'good thing' when it comes to the profitability and ubiquity of companies, but how do you think the government is likely to react? Professor Ian Angell of the London

School of Economics has postulated a number of scenarios that make amusing – or frightening – reading, depending upon your point of view and how much you think they are likely to occur.

What happens, for instance, if transactions 'disappear' into cyberspace with easily identified paper trails of money transfers becoming a thing of the past? We all know of off-shore banking, but where does off-world banking fit in? Come to that, who collects the tax on transactions if there is no geographical boundary that can be associated with a particular business deal? If your business has its HQ in London, manufactures in China, serves a target clientele in the USA and banks in the Cayman Islands, who collects any taxes? And whose tax regime applies?

If governments are unable to trace transactions any longer, then how will they be able to tax them? And if governments can't raise taxes, how will they pay for the infrastructure of their countries? With no infrastructure and social services falling by the wayside, isn't it likely that civil unrest will ensue? And with the division of societies into the 'haves' and the 'have-nots', isn't this a fundamental building block for wars to develop? Spooky stuff, isn't it?

And then, to cap it all, there is the whole issue of VAT. If you decide to buy digitised goods, such as music or software, over the Internet then, in theory, you have to pay VAT if you download them from a server based in the EU. But if that server is based outside the EU, VAT is no longer applicable and you make an immediate saving of 17.5 per cent. (In a similar way, this is why many American companies have set up their e-commerce operations in Delaware since it has no US sales taxes.)

E-commerce has caused a great deal of head scratching in the corridors of power in Brussels. In June 2000 the European Commission published a paper setting out its proposed changes to VAT legislation whereby a non-EU supplier with a turnover of £63,000 a year within the EU would be obliged to register for VAT in a member state of its choice and charge VAT on all taxable supplies.

Now, it just so happens that (at the time of writing) Luxembourg has the lowest VAT rate, set at 15 per cent. So perhaps we will see queues forming up outside Luxembourg's customs and excise offices desperate to register for VAT. And of course the cyber-whiz-kids selling their electronic goods from Massachusetts or Alice Springs are highly likely to insist that their local accountants keep themselves up to date with the changing VAT laws of the EU, aren't they?

This, then, has to be one of the main reasons why Tony Blair's government is risking such unpopularity by pressing ahead with its highly controversial Regulation of Investigatory Powers Bill – known as RIP. Superficially at least, RIP is all about allowing the authorities to crack down on cyber crime through access to encoded material via encryption keys. But even the least cynical must agree that RIP would make it an awful lot easier for the nanny state to keep track of its principle source of revenue.

Transition info Controversy has been re-ignited over e-snooping legislation as only three weeks have been given to companies to respond to a consultation paper on access to employees' e-mail and telephone calls (*Daily Mail*, August 2000).

Transition info The Regulation of Investigatory Powers (RIP) Bill snuck through the Commons like a stealth bomber in fog in February but it has crash-landed in the Lords (*The Sunday Times*, July 2000).

Many companies are genuinely worried that RIP could gravely undermine their own security. If the bill gets Royal Assent it would make Britain the only G8 country apart from Russia with state access to decryption keys. Apart from being a PR disaster for the Labour Party, which many people can live with, many firms are talking openly about leaving Britain if RIP gets the go-ahead – which would seriously undermine Britain's chance of becoming the leading e-industry nation within Europe.

Transition info Censorship has become an Internet headache for China as increasing numbers of people are using it to post opinions on the government and topical issues. However, the government has become just as wired as its critics in checking and tracking any anti-party behaviour.

But governments never learn. Look at Gordon Brown's windfall from the auctioning off of the 3G mobile phone licences. It must have been wonderful for the Exchequer to have raised £22 billion (especially when the Chancellor predicted just one month before the close of bidding that he expected only £2 billion!). But think what a legacy he has created. How will the phone companies recoup their investments, especially when it is highly likely that newer technologies will have been developed by 2004 when these present licences come into their own? Either the charges to end users will be astronomically high, or the companies will go out of business, perhaps being bought up by predators who will leap-frog their efforts to offer something even more sexy to the end users. Once again, time will tell.

There is a huge gap between those who want to regulate the Web and those who actually understand what it is all about. Many an e-commerce guru has torn his hair out at the crass comments that are spouted by those in government who really should know better, but probably never will. There is now a fear that Europe will try to over-regulate, stifling the growth of e-business and handing competitive advantage on a plate to the USA, who in general terms understands this arena much better. Worse still, from UK businesses' point of view, is the tendency of British civil servants to 'gold-plate' the initiatives coming out of Brussels and make them more far-reaching than even the Eurocrats ever envisaged.

> **Foundations** A House of Lords report recommends the creation of an e-ombudsman to handle public grievances over e-commerce, in line with EU moves to set up a formal dispute-resolution service for Internet shoppers.

Meanwhile a number of currency avoidance schemes are being tried (albeit that they may not have been started with that express intention). In the Middle Ages, when bartering schemes were the norm, the only way of working out tax was to assign a nominal value to the goods so that the tax authorities could get their hands on a piece of the action. On the Net you will come across a number of cyber-currencies, of which the best known is Beenz (used in 200,000 transactions a day by over one million customers). Beenz.com has made an arrangement with MasterCard, whereby visitors to more than 300

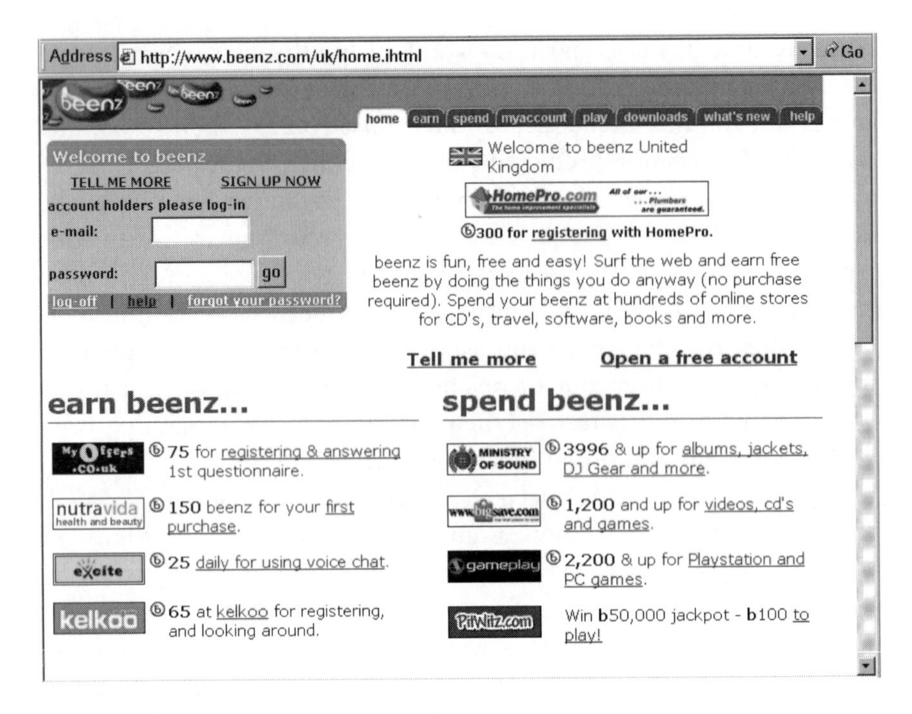

Fig. 22.1 A million housewives every day ...

websites (including household names such as Kingfisher, Excite, MTV, Gameplay and Honda) are paid beenz every time they visit or buy items on-line. The beenz will then be transferred to a special MasterCard debit card that can be used in most shops or on the Net.

Who'd have thought it? There was a wonderful idea dreamt up by an entrepreneur in the early 1990s who decided to pay his staff in gold sovereigns. Each sovereign was worth around £22 on the open market, so he simply 'divided' the salaries he paid his staff by 22 and paid them in sovereigns, whereby they could genuinely declare that they earned $\frac{1}{22}$ of their 'real' worth. (The Inland Revenue soon put a stop to that little scheme!)

Transition info A survey by NOP revealed that more than four million children in the UK use the Internet and growing numbers are clicking on adverts and shopping on-line. The results are likely to accelerate efforts to establish a system of 'children's currency' on-line that will remove some of the barriers to young people using the Internet to shop (*Financial Times*, May 2000)

On-line auctioneer QXL.com has joined forces with Coca-Cola to create a new Internet currency – Coca-Cola ringpulls. Surfers are being encouraged to save their special promotional red ringpulls or labels from cans or bottles to exchange for Coke credits with which they will be able to bid for CDs, computer games, WAP phones and MP3 players over the Internet at the **cokeauction.co.uk** site. There will also be a number of special 'money cannot buy' items, such as having your face and message on the famous Coca-Cola sign in Piccadilly Circus, or playing five-a-side football with members of the England football team.

Chris Banks, MD of Coca-Cola Great Britain, explained that 'the Internet is the most popular forum for young people of all ages. Teens love it, but typically cannot buy things because they do not have credit cards.' QXL is excited because it could stimulate Internet auction bidding to a potential audience of millions.

Now, how long will it take someone in Brussels to work out the number of ringpulls in a euro?

PART 5

FOCUS ON CUSTOMERS AND WHAT THEY *REALLY* WANT

23

CRM – PAST ITS SELL-BY DATE

With all the changes that the Internet has wrought so far, what indications are there of where we might all be going?

Certainly we are fast getting used to the idea of the 'personal portal' – we can personalise our desktops on our computers, select the criteria for e-mailed news services we receive, personalise our televisions with the use of 'favourites', and, of course use mobile phones.

Within the work environment, a personal portal is hosted on an intranet and is simply a Web page that is personalised for each employee. Working teams or groups can also have portals that are specific to the interests of the group. So the personal portal carries information for the person whether it be social, work or interest-based.

Corporate intranets are the largest growth sector in Internet technologies at the moment and are completely metamorphosing business. The increasing demands for the right information to be available throughout an organisation, combined with the pressing need to reduce administration costs by taking advantage of Internet technologies throughout an enterprise, has led to a boom in consultancies devising and implementing these amazing intranets.

It is possible to personalise portals as part of the ultimate streamlining of the intranet, so that people can focus on the areas they want to without the encumbrance of sorting and sifting far greater amounts of information than they would choose.

On the strictly personal level, a personal portal will include a diary, multiple detailed layers of various details such as a map of the local area, car details, registration dates, reminders and all the other things that we carry around in diaries (and palm pilots etc.) at the moment, as well as the other information that is currently on hard copy in filing cabinets at home.

Communications within the personal portal have selection criteria which are perpetually being refined so that e-mails, voice-mail, advertising messages and other correspondence can be barred by the portal owner. Add to this the mobility and personability of mobile phones and you have partially secure mobile portals.

Mobile phones add other dimensions beyond these; with a mobile phone the owner's name, address and financial details are known to the mobile company. Likewise, within a very short space of time, it will not just be who the mobile user is that will be known, but precisely where they are too. We saw in Chapter 20 that global positioning satellites (GPS) can locate you now to within a few metres; as more and more satellites are positioned the location of each mobile user will be able to be pinpointed pretty accurately.

As we mentioned before this could lead to the user being inundated with unwanted advertising messages formulated on the 'think global, act local' mantra. But, in the same way as video recorders can cut out the advertisements, mailing-preference services can reduce junk mail. With the legislation outlawing unwanted e-mail 'spam' already in place, the adman's day of bombarding you with unsolicited missives entreating you to buy products, sign on for services etc. will probably be short-lived.

Push technology, the darling of 1997, was itself short-lived because of the build-up of resentment by the very people at whom it was aimed. People prefer to select information they receive rather than have it pushed at them. However, it will probably live to enjoy another 15 minutes of fame when its refined selection criteria prove more useful than intrusive. And, in the context of finding out local information, 'push' via an SMS message on a portable device could be extremely useful.

The way that the technology is developing and the way it is being used in the converging platforms is leading to smaller and smaller devices that can be used for multiple tasks. So, the mobile phone which has an integral palm device and is WAP and Bluetooth-enabled, will be the sexy tool of the 'noughties'.

We will be able to work in any place at any time. But the mere thought of it leaves a lot of people thoroughly befuddled. Don't let it faze you. Because what it also does is put into the hands of the customer, both corporate and consumer, the power to control the relationship with companies.

So for customer relationship management (CRM) we should now read customer-managed relationships (CMR). The boot is on the other foot – or it will be very shortly. With all that power in the hands of the customer the lot of the company trying to sell products and services is changing.

Picture the scenario where the customer can say 'No!' to receiving your e-mails; 'You're kidding!' to receiving your advertising messages; 'Not you again!' to your promotions. How does this affect how we devise and market our goods and services?

The keys to success in targeting the mobile customer (both corporate and consumer) are *identity*, *interest profile*, *financial profile*, *security* and *location*. Some of these are already known to the mobile phone companies. (They don't have it all, however, as much of this information is still held by special interest groups pertinent to the customer.)

For example, for two years we have been predicting that Vodaphone, or another mobile phone operator, will set up a bank. Imagine if you are on your mobile phone and receive a message that says: 'Would you like to save £20 per month with us? We can offer you a higher rate of interest than anyone else at the moment because we don't have any of the overheads that the others do. If you would like to do this then press "Yes".'

You press 'Yes'.

'Are you sure? Please press "Yes" again to confirm.'

You press 'Yes' again.

They've got the variable direct debit mandate in place that you signed when you agreed the terms of usage for the phone and if they get only 20,000 people agreeing to that little monthly saving then they already have £400,000 per month arriving into their coffers for investment.

Back to CMR. Customers will manage the relationships with your company – and with any others with whom they want to work. The only way for businesses to seek out and then retain customers is to involve them in all the product and service development *as it goes along*.

Internet technologies can facilitate this. Intranets within a company and extranets for suppliers and customers with whom you have special relationships or on whom you are particularly dependent can enable feedback and information transfer. This is the way in which coordination of joint projects is run. And it can be fun.

Many companies will find that they are trying to sell products that customers don't want. Sounds stupid, doesn't it? But it is all too common. A product or service is only any good if it has a ready market rather than a perceived market.

Looking after customers to a greater degree than ever before and ensuring that your whole enterprise is truly focused on the customer and their wants and needs – rather than on how you can get the most money for the least service – will sort the businesses that will survive from those that won't.

Whoops! A customer was disconnected from Breathe's unmetered access deal for 'using it too much' (the *Guardian*, August 2000).

Success will depend on changes in the way that the business works. For instance it is essential that the customer-support people work with marketing and sales. Hiving the customer-support and fulfilment people off to a back room in the traditional way will leave your business limping badly.

Milestones MoneySupermarket has launched its Internet mortgage auction, based on a highly successful American model, but admits it has not been able to return offers to some customers within a guaranteed 48-hour period. High levels of demand sparked by the site's unique proposition – that lenders compete to offer the most attractive mortgage terms – have led to the company hiring triple the number of processing staff and lenders having to work around the

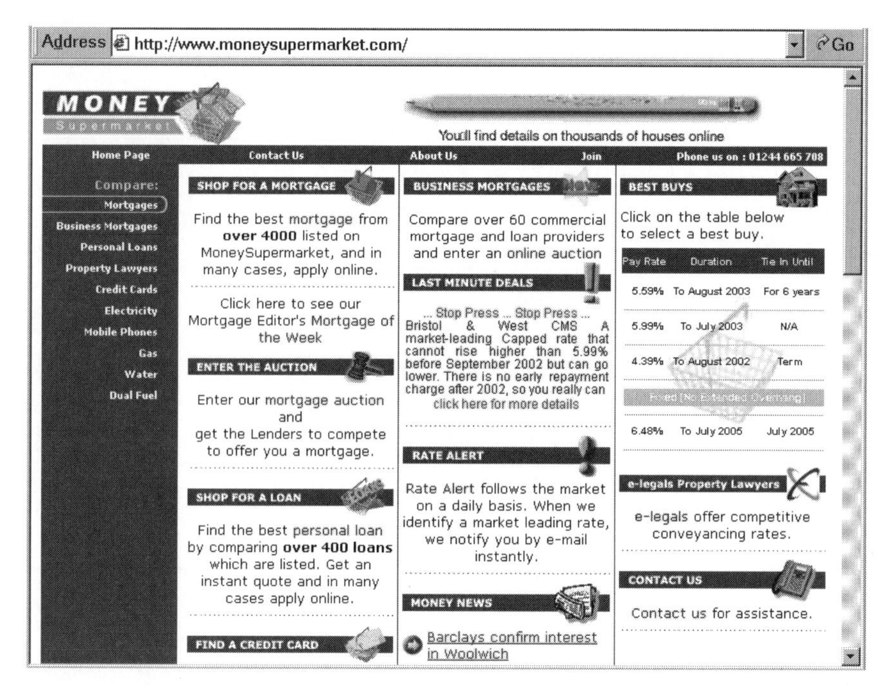

Fig. 23.1 MoneySupermarket has success beyond the dreams of average

clock. The company claims to have £48.5 million of applications for home loans already, and is on track to becoming one of the biggest lenders in the UK by 2001 (the *Independent*, August 2000).

Don't be fooled into thinking that you can continue as before. CRM is now old hat because of the increased power of the customer. Whilst you could think of other ways of managing your customer relations and implement them too, ultimately it is CMR, not CRM, that will win the day.

EPILOGUE

You probably bought this book because you wanted to see if e-commerce would do your company any good. If you haven't gathered by now (or if you jumped ahead to this conclusion) e-commerce is something you won't be able to avoid.

There won't be any Internet companies in five years time. Instead, all companies will use the Internet. If they don't – or try to argue that e-commerce simply isn't for them – they will find that they will become so marginalised that they will die.

Consider what happened when the railways came in, when the telephone reached critical mass, when faxes became a way of business life ... the Internet is becoming ubiquitous in the same way.

So, let's ask the $64,000 question: who takes the biggest risk? Those who do nothing and sit on the sidelines or those who embrace e-commerce and integrate it wholeheartedly into their business? As we have argued throughout this book you have to take part to take advantage of tomorrow's brave new world. And if you don't your company won't be around to take advantage of anything else anyway. After all, big businesses are only small companies that succeeded.

Everyone needs a little time to take a step back and see what those opportunities are in relation to what they are doing at the moment. But don't take too long. The arrival of the Internet has provided the perfect opportunity to allow every business to review their entire *raison d'être*, to plan a viable route map, and to be on track for the future.

You will need to be prepared to be highly flexible and change your plans every two or three months, since timing is critical. Equally, action is essential. There will be no room in business for ostriches.

The Internet is sweeping relentlessly through industry and will ensure change whether you like it or not. Internet technologies are providing the biggest opportunities – and the biggest threats – in your business life.

So, our Parthian shot is: Be vigilant! Look out for the opportunities, watch out for any threats, and focus on the end game.

Index

C